Family Business

·

ASIH SUMARDONO WITH MARK HANUSZ

FAMILY BUSINESS
A Case Study of Nyonya Meneer,
One of Indonesia's Most Successful Traditional Medicine Companies

EQUINOX
PUBLISHING
JAKARTA   KUALA LUMPUR

jointly published by

EQUINOX PUBLISHING (ASIA) PTE. LTD.
No. 3 Shenton Way
#10-05 Shenton House
Singapore 068805
www.EquinoxPublishing.com

and

PT. BUMITRA DAMARDANA
Lippo Plaza 8th floor
Jl. Jend. Sudirman Kav-25
Jakarta Selatan 12920

Family Business:
A Case Study of Nyonya Meneer,
One of Indonesia's Most Successful Traditional Medicine Companies
By Asih Sumardono with Mark Hanusz

ISBN 978-979-3780-58-0

Table of Contents

FOREWORD

I HAVE the pleasure of saying a few words in commemoration of the 88th anniversary of Nyonya Meneer.

I have learned about *jamu* from my grandmother's time. Jamu is indeed a trusted and inseparable part of Indonesia's culture of wellbeing (*budaya sehat*). We all know that the Indonesian archipelago is home to hundreds of varieties of plants, herbs, and spices that have been empirically proven to have medicinal benefits. There are many rare species that can only be found in Indonesia. This gives Indonesia a competitive edge, as jamu is hard to find elsewhere in the world. Hence, jamu is clearly a valuable national asset that can bring pride to the country as well as enhance the economy.

For me, it is interesting to read about the activity of mixing and trying on the efficacy of these plants and using them for numerous purposes from treating a specific illness to preserving general health and beauty. I learn that the production process of jamu is a combination of knowledge and art. With time and experience, a jamu-maker gains a feel for selecting the best materials, the composition of each ingredient, and the best way to blend and process the materials.

Nyonya Meneer, as one of the pioneers in jamu industry, is also one of the first companies committed to producing and distributing jamu. As shown in this book, the company has gone through several metamorphoses, from a sole woman entrepreneur producing and delivering her products by hand to become a first-rate company marketing jamu worldwide.

It is my hope that this book, which charts the journey of one of Indonesia's most successful traditional medicine companies, can provide insight and inspiration to other companies interested in exploring this precious national treasure and realize its market potential. In this publication, one can find an honest account of the difficulties faced and trials overcame in Nyonya Meneer's experience in building its company from modest beginnings to international stature. What makes it even more compelling, the book concludes with still more challenges that the jamu industry must confront in the future.

Mari Elka Pangestu
Minister of Trade, Republic of Indonesia
Jakarta, 20 July 2007

INTRODUCTION

❧

INDONESIA IS a land rich with hundreds of varieties of spices and medicinal plants – and perhaps hundreds more are yet to be discovered. These coveted spices, such as pepper, clove, and nutmeg, are the reason Columbus went in search for the New World and New Amsterdam changed its name to New York. Naturally, this wealth of indigenous plants has made its way into Indonesian traditional remedies after centuries of experimentation and usage. It should also be no surprise that entrepreneurial individuals have developed world-class companies producing this traditional medicine. What is a surprise, though, is how popular this medicine is for tens of millions of Indonesians and how little it is known in other countries.

The traditional medicine is known locally as *jamu*. There is no direct translation into English except for awkward phrases like "traditional medicine" or "herbal remedy," which are insufficient as jamu combines complex, often secret formulas involving tens of different ingredients and is used to treat ailments ranging from rheumatism to poor blood circulation to impotence. Although each jamu is primarily designed to treat one specific illness, the same jamu can often cure a range of other ailments as it works on holistic principles. However, its healing process takes longer to produce results compared to synthetic medicine. Nevertheless, while jamu is not an "instant" cure, research has shown its contra-indications are considerably less than pharmaceuticals, which contain chemical substances.

At first, these jamu recipes were passed down orally, some special ones were even immortalized in songs and chants, such as those found in *Serat Centini*. In the 19th century, some of these recipes were collected in manuscripts. However, it doesn't mean that anyone can follow these recipes and make great jamu. Different jamu-makers can come up with different quality, flavor, and scent with the same recipe. Moreover, each ethnic group has different ways in preparing these remedies. Certain jamu became identified with certain areas as the ingredients could only grow in that part of the world. The soil, the climate, the air, everything makes a difference in the quality of the plants grown and, consequently, the jamu produced. For example, Indonesia has some of the world's best *temulawak* (round turmeric rhizomes) that prevents hepatitis and cancer, as well as the best ginger. There are also many rare species that can only be found in Indonesia. Thus, jamu can be the area's local signature product. All this makes jamu a national treasure that also has great commercial potential.

Conventionally, jamu is sold door-to-door. In the mornings or late afternoons, people in their houses would hear the calls of *Mbok Jamu* – the usual nickname for the woman jamu-seller. You can see her in most residential areas, usually wearing *kebaya*, the Indonesian traditional jacket blouse, and carrying a basket on her back containing bottles of jamu solutions in various colors. She would call out to prospective customers in a distinctive way, "*Jamu… jamu… Jamunya,*

Bu!" (Jamu...jamu...would you buy jamu, Ma'am?") Then customers would come out of their houses, call her, and let her in to their front porch and buy glassfuls of jamu. This scene is very familiar for most Indonesians – especially Javanese.

The manufacturing of jamu as an industry first developed in Java in the early twentieth century. Nyonya Meneer, the subject of this case study, is one of the first companies that existed. Today, similar to the other indigenous Indonesian product, *kretek* or clove cigarettes, jamu is produced by hundreds of companies ranging from industrial conglomerates to home industry. Some companies have hundreds of products, some have only one. The range and diversity of their products are as wide as the companies themselves.

Each jamu company has its own stories to tell, but because most are family-owned, one tends not to hear too much about the inner workings, much less the intrigues they face throughout the generations. This book, *Family Business*, is the inside story of the history of one of the country's largest companies, Semarang-based Nyonya Meneer.

From humble beginnings 88 years ago in the back of the founder's house to a conglomerate producing over two hundred types of jamu and cosmetics and selling all over Indonesia and in more than a dozen countries, Nyonya Meneer certainly has had its share of triumphs and tragedies. And unlike most family-owned companies that would prefer to keep their business private, the story of Nyonya Meneer is now exposed to the world. I hope you find the story as fascinating as I have.

Mark Hanusz
Jakarta, 8 August 2007

FAMILY BUSINESS

CHAPTER ONE

IN THE BEGINNING

❦

In August 1895, a girl was born in a small town of Sidoarjo in the province of East Java to Tjoe Hwa Nio. She was named Lauw Ping Nio, but because her mother continually craved for *menir*, or soft rice grains, throughout her pregnancy, Ping Nio was given the nickname *Menir*, which turned into Noni Meneer, or Miss Meneer (using the Dutch spelling at the time) during her childhood.

As a girl growing up during the Dutch administration in the Netherlands Indies, Noni Meneer was not allowed to attend school. Thus, her mother, in addition to teaching her household skills, invited a teacher to come to their house to teach her how to read and write. Her mother also taught her the art of using natural ingredients to make medicinal tonics to cure ailments like colds and rheumatic pains.

When she was seventeen years old, a businessman from nearby Surabaya named Ong Bian Wan proposed to her. As was common at the time, Noni Meneer didn't even meet her husband-to-be, and everything was arranged by her parents. After they were married, Noni

Meneer came to be called Nyonya (or Mrs.) Meneer. Shortly after their marriage, the couple moved to Semarang to explore new business opportunities for Bian Wan. Nyonya Meneer diligently performed her duties as a wife and bore children.

After several years of marriage, Bian Wan was overcome by a stomach ailment that forced him to stay in bed. Nyonya Meneer visited all the doctors in Semarang but could not find a way to bring comfort to her ill husband. Recalling what her mother taught her when she was a girl, Nyonya Meneer blended a traditional Javanese tonic and gave it to her husband every day for one month. Miraculously, after one month Bian Wan's stomach pain disappeared.

The news of Bian Wan's full recovery quickly spread around Semarang. Soon after neighbors began to visit Nyonya Meneer asking to try her tonics. Nyonya Meneer obliged, and developed formulas for curing of the most common ailments, all the time managing the household and raising her three children, Nonie, Hans Ramana, and Lucie, and teaching the same skills she learned from her own mother.

When Nyonya Meneer was pregnant with her fourth child, Bian Wan's ailment came back and no matter how many different potions she tried, he was unable to recover and passed away. She became determined to not only improve her own tonics, but also to make a business out of it to support her family. She began to buy raw materials and hire assistants to blend the herbs and spices.

A few months later, her fourth child, Marie, was born. Nyonya Meneer was as determined as ever to continue growing the business, while giving full attention to her children. Word of her tonics began to spread outside of Semarang as well. In the early days, Nyonya Meneer would deliver the tonic directly to the customers, and the customers felt that this hand-delivery was a key ingredient in the efficacy of the tonic itself. After a while she realized that it wasn't practical to supervise the mixing of ingredients *and* hand-deliver the final product to the customer, so she devised an idea that let her remain in Semarang but still keep the customers happy: she put a photo of herself on the label. This was an unusual practice at the time as the labels were quite expensive to print, but she was convinced this was the only way she could expand her business and keep her customers' trust and loyalty. She also hired a full-time sales manager to promote and sell her tonic around the Semarang area.

A few years later, Nyonya Meneer met a gentleman named Nio Tek An and she decided it was time to marry again. Soon thereafter her fifth child was born, Hans Pangemanan.

Her house in Semarang soon became overcrowded with children, staff and raw materials so she decided to open a retail store in Semarang's main shopping area: Pedamaran Market. She found an ideal location at Jl. Pedamaran no. 92 and built a counter where customers could either consume the tonic directly in her shop or take it home. Her tonic powders included the intestinal medicine her first husband used, as well as various other blends for general health. She appointed two of her daughters, Marie and Lucie, to mind the shop after school.

Nyonya Meneer focused on developing more tonics and learning about the different properties of medicinal plants and herbs. Her laboratory was in her house on Jl. Raden Patah no. 195 and was filled with the aroma of these plants and herbs. From morning until night she mixed herbs with a mortar and pestle, and roasted roots and leaves in an iron skillet. Her assistants would help with the preparation of the plants and herbs. The house was a beehive of activity, constantly providing a wider and wider range of products to sell in her shop. Her children were always nearby, learning how to mix the herbs just like Nyonya Meneer learned from her own mother. After the children went to sleep, she diligently prepared the budget for purchasing of raw materials, devised new recipes and ways to bring these products to market.

After a while, Nyonya Meneer became the head of a rapidly expanding business without even realizing it. She supervised all research and development, human resources, purchasing, marketing, and selling. She hired commissioned agents to represent her products outside of Semarang in Cirebon, Yogyakarta and Solo. By 1940, at the age of 45, she had sixteen employees and still managed to look after her five children.

As the business began to become profitable, she did not hesitate to share the profits among the employees. She provided them with bonuses and kept her employees motivated to stay loyal and productive. Nyonya Meneer also began preparing for her company's future by sending her eldest son, Hans Ramana, to Hong Kong to study engineering in 1941. Unfortunately for Hans, shortly after he arrived in Hong Kong, World War II broke out. Since this took a drastic toll on the company's finances, Nyonya Meneer was unable to continue providing funding for Hans. He was forced to abandon his studies, moved to Beijing, and started a new career: as a soldier in Chiang Kai-Shek's army. After the war, Hans sent a telegram to his mother telling her that he was coming home.

Hans arrived back in Indonesia in 1946 and moved to Jakarta, the capital city, to live with his eldest sister, Nonie, who by that time was in charge of distribution of Nyonya Meneer's jamu there. Nonie's base of operations was on Jl. Juanda in the Pasar Baru market district, and business was growing swiftly. On a chance occasion, one of Hans's cousins introduced him to a lovely lady named Vera, and he immediately fell in love. He shot off another telegram to his mother to tell her the good news, only to discover that Nyonya Meneer herself was actively looking for a wife for Hans back in Semarang. After some initial confusion – and a heartbreak or two – Hans and Vera married in Semarang in 1947. One condition Nyonya Meneer placed on Hans was that he would join the company after the wedding, and his first posting was in Bandung to open distribution of jamu in West Java.

Hans and Vera had four children, and the first two, Benita and Gwyneth were born during his tour of duty in Semarang. In 1951 Nyonya Meneer recalled Hans back to Semarang to take over the business, and there they had their other two children, Charles and Fiona.

Beginning in 1950, Nyonya Meneer decided it was time to properly establish a legal company. Until that time, she has operated as a home industry but the business had gotten too big. She hired an accountant to clean up the books and hired a notary to begin the process of legalizing her operations. The process was completed in 1952 and Nyonya Meneer became known as CV (*Commanditaire Vernootschap* or limited partnership) Nyonya Meneer, and it confirmed her place as Indonesia's first woman entrepreneur.

She then appointed her daughters Lucie and Marie as commissioners, and named her first son, Hans Ramana as President Director. It is now his responsibility to lead the company and ensure it would thrive in the second generation of management.

One of Hans's first acts as President Director was to purchase a grinding machine from Germany to increase productivity one hundred-fold. Work that would normally take three days would only take one hour with the new machine. With this new capacity, Nyonya Meneer could concentrate on developing even more products for her expanding customer base. Whenever one of her children or a neighbor would get sick, she would prepare a test batch of her new formulas. Sometimes they worked, sometimes not – but she always kept detailed records and constantly improved on the formula.

Nyonya Meneer was convinced that tonics were simply more effective than a standard doctor prescription. She reasoned a doctor's pill normally contained four to five different active ingredients, but her tonics often contained more than twenty-five. Fortunately, Indonesia's reputation as home of the Spice Islands ensured she would never run out of raw material and new, interesting ingredients.

She discovered that certain spices should be treated according to their use. Some should be completely dried, while other spices only needed to be half dried. Each ingredient should be ground in its own grinder so the herbs wouldn't contain traces of another. She controlled the sensitivity of the tonic powders – some should be completely smooth and others should be rough. She personally monitored every aspect of production from raw material selection to storing to blending to even packaging.

Despite keeping a close eye on the business, she nevertheless gave her children authority to manage the company without interference. Nonie was still in charge of Jakarta distribution, Marie was Finance Director, Lucie was Production Director, her youngest son, Hans Pangemanan was in the marketing department, and everyone reported to Hans Ramana as President Director. Keeping with her mother-figure role, she continued to coach her children and treat the company's employees with dignity and respect, and taught them to be disciplined and motivated. During the 1950s and 1960s, CV Nyonya Meneer expanded from a minor player in the traditional medicine industry to one of its largest.

As a result of the company's good fortune and proven sustainability, Nyonya Meneer formally divided the company into shares and dispersed them among her children. Out of 200 shares, Hans Ramana received 50, Hans Pangemanan received 50, Lucie received 35, Marie received 35, Nonie received 10, and Nyonya Meneer held the remaining 20.

In 1967, Hans Ramana bought a house in Jakarta's elite district of Menteng for Vera and his family. Vera had moved to Jakarta years earlier as she found Semarang too provincial. That same year, Hans's eldest daughter, Benita, moved to Melbourne. In 1972, Benita moved to New York where he got a job working for PanAm airlines and was transferred to Honolulu in 1974.

In the early 1970s Hans felt it was time to diversify the company's product range. While traditionally Nyonya Meneer had focused on herbal medicine and tonics, Hans added a range of beauty products like hair cream and massage oil. One of the main reasons for this was at the time several new jamu companies were entering the market and selling their jamu at a deep discount to Nyonya Meneer's. Fortunately, the company and its products had such a good reputation with its customers that even though they might try a competitor's products, they usually came back to the trusted Nyonya Meneer brand.

After decades of uninterrupted growth for the company, the possibility of problems occurring was much more of a *when* than an *if*. In December 1975, Hans Ramana, President Director of Nyonya Meneer for 23 years, was diagnosed with cancer. The cancer was at such an advanced stage that immediate action had to be taken. Benita was stationed in Hawaii and insisted he be brought there for treatment. Using a compassionate leave pass from PanAm, Benita flew to Jakarta in January 1976 to escort her ailing father to Queen's Hospital in Honolulu. On arrival, the attending physician concurred with the diagnosis of cancer, and he informed the family that as the cancer was at such an advanced stage, treatment was not possible. For weeks there was a steady stream of children, uncles and aunts coming all the way from Indonesia to be with Hans at his bedside. Just as the entire family bonded together during this difficult time, Hans Ramana passed away on February 14, 1976. As Hans last memories were in the Hawaii he loved so much, the family chose to bury him in the Valley of the Temples cemetery.

Back in Semarang, the second tragedy was unfolding. Six months prior to Hans's death, Nyonya Meneer had a stroke and developed difficulties in speaking as well as in her long-term memory. After much consideration, the children decided it was best to keep the sickness and death of her beloved son secret as the news would certainly cause her own health to worsen even further. Instinctively, she knew something was wrong as there were no more letters or phone calls from Hans, but the children were resolute in keeping the secret from her.

The death of Hans Ramana brought several management changes to the company. Weeks before he died, Hans asked his eldest son, Charles Saerang – who was studying business in the US at the time – to return to Indonesia and help the family run the company. As Charles was only 24 at the time, it was decided he would be nominated a commissioner with his aunts Marie and Lucie, while his aunt Nonie was appointed President Director and his uncle Hans Pangemanan became Vice President Director.

In 1978, Nyonya Meneer decided to visit her grandchildren who were studying in Australia. Her daughter Marie had flown to Jakarta to get her visa, and she was scheduled to depart on April 24. That afternoon, Nyonya Meneer developed chest pains and was short of breath. A doctor was summoned, and he advised she should be hospitalized immediately. She refused, insisting to stay in her house with her children and grandchildren. The doctor gave her an I.V. and oxygen tube, but a few hours later her heart stopped and she passed away in her sleep.

Nyonya Meneer, Indonesia's first and one of its most successful female entrepreneurs and one of the founders of the Indonesia's jamu industry, passed away at the age of 83. She left behind a strong and innovative company with four children and one grandson at the helm. While she was alive, the company had enjoyed years of steady growth without any management conflicts. Unfortunately, her death would change all of that.

The iconic picture of Nyonya Meneer, which became the company's logo. The outfit, sandals, and jewelry she wore in the picture are displayed at the Jamu Museum at Jalan Kaligawe, Semarang.

*Nyonya Meneer with her husband and children at the front yard of their house,
Jalan Raden Patah no.195, Semarang (circa 1930).*

Nyonya Meneer with her children and grandchildren at the back of her house,
at the area used to dry raw materials (circa 1950).
Nyonya Meneer is the older woman in center left; to her right is her grandson
Carel Oei (son of Nonie and Oke Saerang) and his wife.

Nyonya Meneer supervising workers making jamu at her house (circa 1950).

Nyonya Meneer with her children and grandchildren at her birthday party (circa 1950).

Nyonya Meneer with her children and their future spouses (circa 1955).
Sitting down from left: Ella Pangemanan, Vera Saerang, Nonie Saerang,
Nyonya Meneer, Lucie Saerang and Marie Kalalo.
Standing from left: Hans Pangemanan, Hans Ramana, Oke Saerang,
Choa Hie Hian, and Ong Hien Sin. After many internal conflicts and struggles,
only one family would hold the shares of the company, that of Hans Ramana and Vera Saerang.

Nyonya Meneer at her 59th birthday celebration at her house (1954).

The family of Hans Ramana, Nyonya Meneer's first-born son (circa 1963).
Standing from left to right: Charles, Benita. Sitting down from
left to right: Gwyneth, Fiona Oni, Vera Saerang, and Hans Ramana.

Three grandchildren of Nyonya Meneer from her son, Hans Ramana, the company's first President Director. From left to right: Benita, Charles, and Gwyneth (circa 1957).

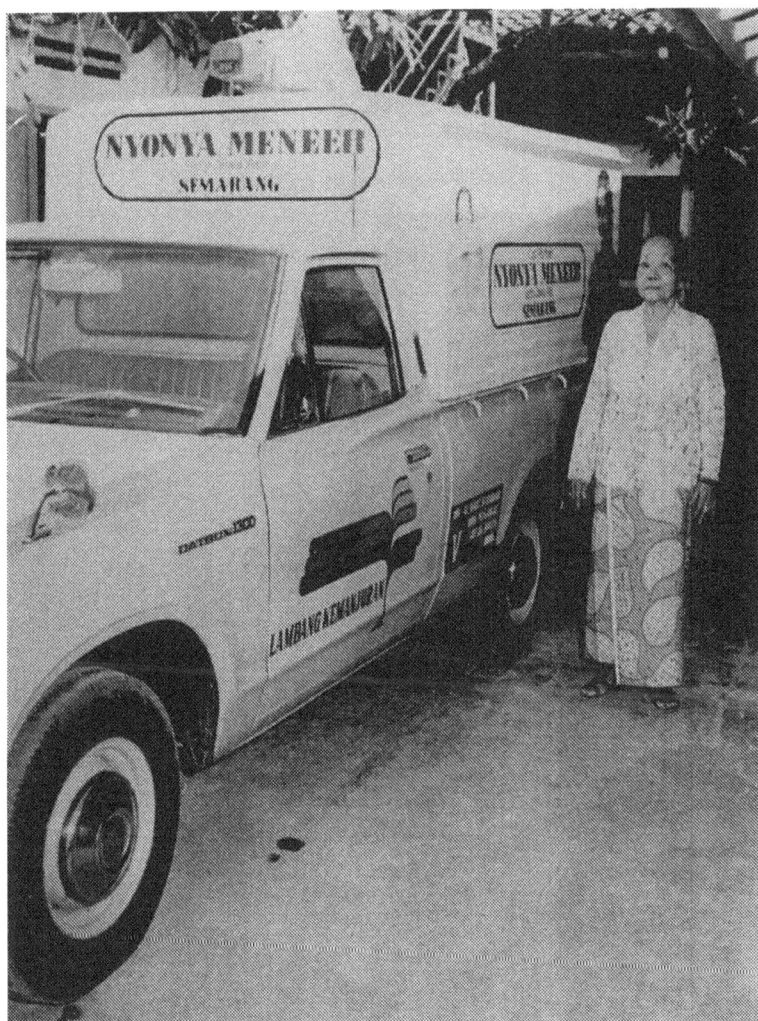

*Nyonya Meneer's first delivery truck that marked the beginning of the company's
vast expansion in marketing and distribution (circa 1960).*

The old factory at Jalan Raden Patah no.190. In its place now stands the head office (called Gedung Multiguna 2020) *and the new factory – built adjacent to Nyonya Meneer's house (circa 1980).*

Various herbs used in Nyonya Meneer's jamu

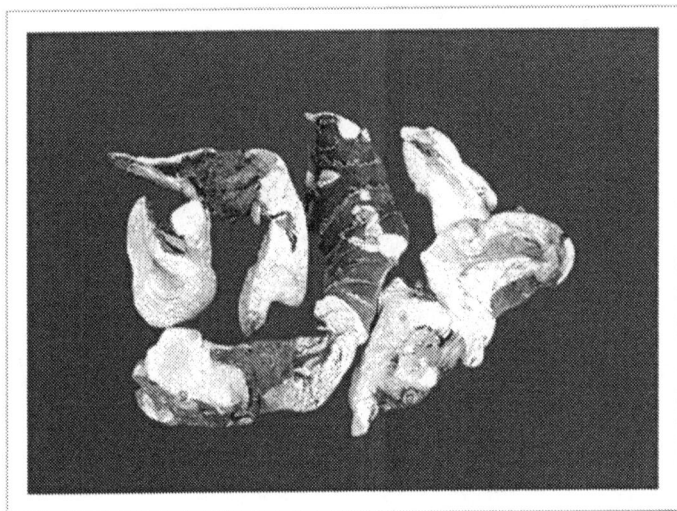

Rimpang jahe (Zingiberis rhizoma)

Rimpang lengkuas (Languatis rhizoma)

Daun kejibeling (Sericocalycis folium)

Buah kapulaga (Amomi fructus)

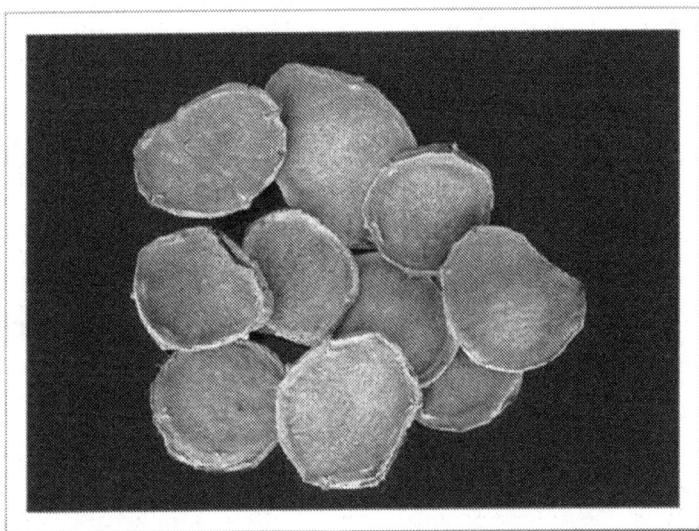

Rimpang temulawak (Curcumae rhizoma)

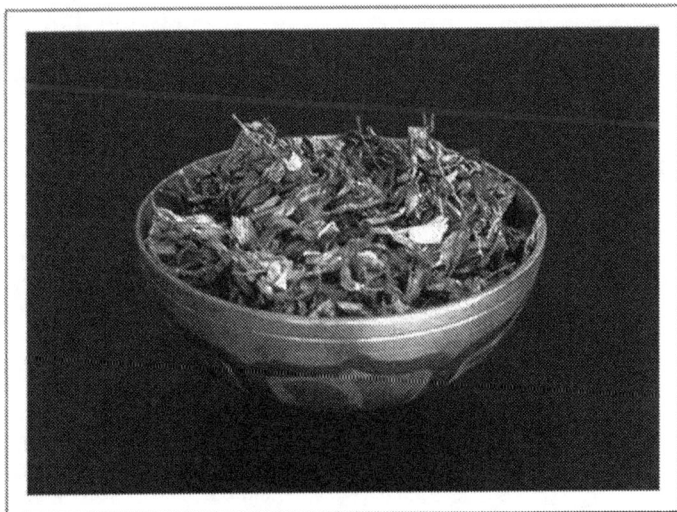

Bunga Sidawayah (Woodfordiae flos)

The first printed jamu packaging made from paper (*circa* 1940). The current packaging with the company's signature three-partite design came out in the early 1970s.

Djamu Djanoko, a jamu that boosts strength for men.

Djamu Kuat Raksasa, (jamu for gigantic strength) for men "with weak bodies" and little energy.

Djamu Njamnir, to maintain health and freshness in women's bodies.

Djamu Patmosari, a jamu for women to keep the body beautiful.

Portrait of Nyonya Meneer by the acclaimed painter Raden Basoeki Abdullah (circa 1980).

CHAPTER TWO
THE FIRST CRISIS

NOW THAT the management of PT Nyonya Meneer had passed to its second generation, the attention of the family focused on young Charles, who had just returned to Indonesia at the request of his dying father.

Charles was born in Semarang, on February 20, 1952, the third child of Hans Ramana and Vera Saerang. They lived at the family compound on Jl. Raden Patah and after primary school, Charles moved to Jakarta with his parents. Charles was considered shy and introverted, and dreamed of leaving Indonesia to study abroad. When Charles asked his father for permission, Hans Ramana gave it without even asking what he was intending to study. His mother, on the other hand, rejected the idea remarking, "You can't even speak English. You'll only get yourself into trouble." Over time, Charles managed to convince his mother that this was his destiny, and in 1968 both parents gave their blessing to continue his studies in London. He was sixteen years old.

Charles was admitted to the London Academy, and a school friend, Tino Natawidjaya, joined him for the journey. The school was strict and enforced a strong discipline on him. His classmates were from all over the world: China, Turkey, Pakistan, Thailand – and Charles was the only Indonesian. At the beginning, English was his biggest problem. He studied hard to keep up with his friends who spoke good English, and read many English-language books. The language barrier slowly began to disappear.

During the school holidays, he kept himself busy traveling around London and the countryside. He stayed with a family in Eastbourne where he paid for bed and breakfast, and was only allowed to use the bathroom once a week. In London, he worked at a friend's Indonesian restaurant as a waiter and cook. Far removed from his privileged life-style in Semarang, Charles learned the lesson of hard work.

In 1970 Charles transferred to Acton Technical College in Hammersmith for his A levels. Since he was a boy, he wanted to be a doctor and thus he took zoology and chemistry. Unfortunately, he failed both and for a short time contemplated returning to Indonesia. He decided that if he did that, he would consider this incredible opportunity a failure. One day he noticed an advertisement for a counseling session on vocational guidance. It was a four-hour exam, and the results said he was most qualified to become a priest, politician or marketing guru. At the time in Indonesia, ethnic Chinese were more or less forbidden to enter politics, and he couldn't imagine becoming a priest. So he chose the third option and moved to the country that was considered at the forefront of business education: The United States.

Charles's first stop was in Nashville, Tennessee where he enrolled in Middle Tennessee State University. Apparently the marketing stud-ies suited him and he finished the first year at the top of his class and then decided to enroll in a more specialized business management program. He chose Miami University in Oxford, Ohio to continue his management and marketing studies. After two years and nearly finished with his degree, Charles received a phone call: Your father is dying. You need to come back to Indonesia.

Charles nearly took the first plane back, but he was informed by the university that final exams were just a couple of weeks away and they could not be postponed. Charles had comfort in the fact that his eldest sister Benita would be taking care of their father in Hawaii so he could focus on his critical studies, just as his father would have wanted. He spoke with his father on the phone, and on his deathbed Hans asked Charles to promise him he would come home and assist his Aunt Marie. Even though Charles was looking forward to a career in the US, he agreed. Two months later, after his father passed away, Charles received his Bachelor of Science degree from Miami University and prepared to move back to Indonesia.

By the end of 1976, Charles was back in Semarang and in keeping with his promise to his father, he started his career in the company's marketing department. He knew that he had to tread carefully; even though he had a degree in business from a prestigious American university, he was still 24 years old and his aunts and uncles were going to keep a watchful eye over him. His suggestions and ideas were originally met with skepticism; how can this young man know anything about the company we have been managing for years? He thought strategically how he could make the company grow, but the rest of the family seemed only interested in how to make short-term profits at a long-term expense.

For two years, Charles hit the road and visited all of the company's agents around the country – especially those in remote areas. He reasoned that in order to improve sales, he first had to figure out the current situation. He traveled by car, motorcycle or sometimes even on foot throughout Indonesia. He shared personal stories with his agents and established trust so that they would be completely open and honest with him.

He was shocked to discover how the agents were notoriously marking up the prices of the jamu, and therefore pricing them out of the market. The conflict was Charles was interested in volume and market share, and the agents were only concerned about fat margins. Also, he noticed the company's distribution network was slow and inefficient. "What good is product promotion if the distribution system is not effectual?" Charles asked himself. So before Charles could improve the marketing of the company's products, it became crystal clear he had to work out the distribution issues first.

A strong and proven distribution network must be based on a strong foundation. To build this foundation, both the company and its distributors had to trust each other. Nyonya Meneer instigated a program of loans to distributors to improve and expand their network. Also, the company shared their marketing research and knowledge with the distributors, and gave them the freedom to develop themselves without outside interference. Nyonya Meneer also invited its agents and distributors on trips to Hong Kong and Japan to study other ways of distributing products around the country.

Charles became the de facto marketing teacher for the company's distributors. With a proper and efficient distribution network in place, the market will enlarge and the company will be inspired to develop new and innovative promotional strategies based on this new customer awareness. If these promotions are then effective, and the distribution efficient, both company and distributor will grow rapidly.

The other shift in company-distributor relations came in the form of trusting the local distributors to know their market. Whereas before the company didn't allow the distributors to deviate from the company's defined marketing strategy, Charles gave his sellers full authority to develop their business in their marketing area. Instead of the company treating its distributors as employees, they began to treat them as business partners.

Within one year of this improvement of the distribution network, sales doubled.

In the years after Hans Ramana and Nyonya Meneer died, other problems within the company became apparent. The once legendary quality control she demanded for all of her products started to fade. Many products were shipped damaged or continued to be sold beyond their expiration date. The risk of a permanent damage to Nyonya Meneer's reputation loomed large. Moreover, the products that the company did produce were not marketed effectively and often not responsive to market conditions. With the distribution network vastly improved and the company's products smoothly making their way to all points of the archipelago, Charles thought it was time to improve the company's promotions. In 1980, as a result of his reorganizing and revitalizing of Nyonya Meneer's distribution network, he was promoted to Director of Marketing. And he was eager to finally put all of his education to use for his grandmother's company.

In the early 1980s, there was intense competition in both the jamu and the pharmaceutical industries. Urban areas were shifting from traditional remedies and instead consuming more of the doctor-prescribed conventional kind. Charles realized that there was an important education that needed to take place: teaching Indonesian consumers about their own traditional remedies before they were entirely forgotten.

This education process could be done in many ways: newspapers, magazines, product placement in movies and radio, etc. At that time, no jamu manufacturer had any interest in advertising their products.

It just wasn't common; sales relied on word-of-mouth promotion and national campaigns were unheard of. Seizing this opportunity, Nyonya Meneer embarked on a massive, nation-wide publicity campaign for all of their products.

Charles hired the father of Indonesian pop music, Nomo Koeswoyo, to develop a jingle for the company (it became so popular that most Indonesians born before 1970 can still remember it). He sponsored concerts by the legendary band, Koes Plus, and tickets sold out so fast he had to hire police to control the crowds. He was the first to place a full-color ad in newspapers as well as was the first to advertise on radio and TV. Charles told his aunt Nonie he needed to change the name of one of their products, Jamu Senin Kamis (Monday Thursday) to Awet Ayu (Everlasting Beauty). He believed in the efficacy of the product, but it was only selling 1000 packs a month. While Awet Ayu product would have exactly the same ingredients and the same segmentation, target, and positioning, he was convinced that with a more alluring name and prettier packaging he would increase sales. He developed a campaign with S. Djalil from Adforce, one of the country's most renowned advertising agencies. After six months of the new Awet Ayu campaign, sales exceeded 800,000 per month.

CASE STUDY ONE: AWET AYU
(see The Evolution of Awet Ayu Advertisements in pages 67-72)

In the 1980s, almost all the existing jamu companies sold similar products whose purpose was to treat an illness rather than the body. For example, it was clear these companies were marketing jamu as a cure for headaches and were not interested in selling jamu to women as a beauty-aid.

Therefore, a golden opportunity existed to introduce products for beauty- and body-care. Nyonya Meneer understood that women were very much interested in looking after their bodies. Many women prized a beautiful and elegant look above all else, making beauty treatments their first priority. Moreover, Indonesian women were already so familiar with jamu; it had become a part of their daily lives. They were introduced to jamu as early as when they were toddlers. As they grow up and start getting period, there is also a jamu product for them. After they marry, there is jamu promoting sexual intimacy. When they have children, there is jamu to help with delivery and breast-feeding. As they grow old, there is jamu to halt the hands of time. It seemed that Nyonya Meneer made an excellent decision in creating a range of product that specifically target women as consumers.

Since then Nyonya Meneer has conducted a great deal of research into women's beauty products. Out of all the jamu, Awet Ayu proved the perfect product for this new market. Awet Ayu cosmetics are a natural beauty treatment whose formulae were created specifically for the tropical Indonesian climate.

The right time and opportunity came together and opened the door for product modification. During the development stages, Nyonya Meneer produced Awet Ayu in the form of pills, tablets, liquid, and capsules. Then, they launched Awet Ayu body soap for those not familiar with using powder to clean the skin. The various versions of Awet Ayu were made without changing the basic ingredients of the jamu. With such a wide choice, there was no reason for women to reject the Awet Ayu range. Furthermore, Awet Ayu had been tested by the Ministry of Health laboratory, supervised by the Food and Drugs Supervisory Council (*Badan Pengawas Obat dan Makanan* – BPOM) confirming Awet Ayu was safe.

Good planning enabled the marketing manager to launch a series of Awet Ayu products in 1978 together with tips on how to use it success-fully. The marketing department identified its target audience before starting a major promotional campaign in all the print and electronic media. The Awet Ayu commercials featured a catchy jingle at the time that was soon familiar to the public. People saw this promotion in many different places: while they were reading magazines and news-papers, watching television, in cinemas as well as on billboards at stra-tegic street corners where there was heavy pedestrian traffic. It was considered a strong move that had never been implemented by any other jamu company in the same market.

It was essential to allocate funds accurately to carry out this pro-motion. The family thought promotional activities were a waste of money. However, the marketing department was keen to run it be-cause they were optimistic about the results and feedback they would receive in the future. They were determined to go ahead as they esti-mated all the costs could be recouped and profits would exceed the target figure.

The expectation was fulfilled. Within a short space of time the public could identify the Awet Ayu range. Promoting a product through advertising was considered a new departure and inspired the whole industry. Advertising was found to be extremely effective for marketing products. Just imagine no one knew about Awet Ayu, its function, ingredients or how it should be used. Previously consumers had never been attracted to the product and the warehouse was piled high with stock because it wasn't selling. But after the promotions, Awet Ayu beat hundreds of other Nyonya Meneer products to become its bestseller.

Promotion and information spread by the advertisements had lured consumers to the retail outlets and Awet Ayu's pretty packaging also tempted them. It featured a beautiful long-haired model relating her experience of the product. Awet Ayu grabbed consumer's attention and they bought the products in droves. Alicia Johar, one of the popular actresses in the 1980s, was used as the model.

Another promotional activity was conducting seminars at various women's organizations. A demonstration was included showing a complete body treatment. Charles Saerang explained the use and function of Awet Ayu at almost all the seminars to increase customer satisfaction. A strong relationship could only be built through dialogue between the manufacturer and customer to give them good information on the products. In the print media, advertisements not only showed the picture of a beautiful woman using the product, but magazines and newspapers printed articles as well as question and answer sections. An interactive dialogue was launched on radio to promote body treatments using Awet Ayu products. The media provided customers with many opportunities to call with their beauty queries. Thus, readers of newspapers, magazines and those listening to the radio received accurate solutions to their problems.

The barrage of information caught the customers' attention; women wanted to find out if this product could live up to its claims. Thousands of them rushed to the shops to buy Awet Ayu. Educating customers about the range and proving it was effective soon turned them into fanatic consumers. This resulted in a bond being formed between consumer and producer. Market demand for the Awet Ayu range automatically increased. The campaign proved that using advertising to highlight the benefits promised by Awet Ayu had a knock-on effect and substantially increased profits of other Nyonya Meneer lines.

The huge consumer response to the body treatment products made Awet Ayu the top product for six months. Women seemed obsessed with using the products. As the result, the company had difficulty meeting demand and every production run would be sold out the next day. This gave rise to the joke that people could only buy the advertisement because the products were permanently sold out. Awet Ayu made Nyonya Meneer very popular. As a result of this success the family company that was initially profit-oriented was transformed into one that was market-oriented.

Coincidentally, the success of Awet Ayu had a great effect on the stagnating jamu industry. It created competition among jamu companies as to which one could supply the best product to the consumer. This was evident when another jamu company adopted Nyonya Meneer's marketing strategy. Some competitors, who had previously underestimated Nyonya Meneer began to acknowledge the excellent work of the marketing manager in identifying precisely what consumers wanted. They soon started to watch each step taken by Nyonya Meneer very carefully as they did not want to be left behind again!

The success of Awet Ayu sales raised Nyonya Meneer's jamu to the highest level. As the biggest, most innovative jamu company in Indonesia, Nyonya Meneer was aware that consumer needs were of the utmost importance and as producers they must not be complacent. To allow this product to survive and strive for continuous improvement, they must find other products with the same potential.

In the mid-1990s, the company expanded the range of Awet Ayu products. They began by adding different varieties to the Awet Ayu category and went on to reshape the product by introducing it in more practical forms. As the result, Awet Ayu had a long list of benefits such as: removing body odor with the addition of *beluntas* plant essence (*Plucheae Indicae foliae*), *temulawak* (*Curcumae rhizoma*), and turmeric (*Curcumae domesticae rhizoma*) to reduce the size of pores and prevent the skin sweating excessively.

The increasing demand for cosmetics around the world pushed jamu companies to open up markets in the West. It quickly became clear that beauty products sold well in European countries but the priority was to sell these alongside jamu. As the range was developed, Awet Ayu products always progressed and improved in line with consumer needs. Quality was meticulously monitored to gain consumer trust. In 1994, these products were seen in one of France's respected beauty institutions. The outrageous costs seemed to be offset by the increased demand in world markets. Even today Awet Ayu remains the mainstay of Nyonya Meneer.

Nyonya Meneer has always tried to realize consumer desires and tastes that moved with time. Accordingly the company created a series of modern cosmetics made from natural ingredients, which had gone through research and monitoring process in the laboratory of the World Cosmetic Centre to achieve perfection and quality of the best natural product.

When Charles returned to America to study for his doctorate, the success of Awet Ayu in the market inspired him to use the case history for his dissertation, which was eventually entitled *Jamu Awet Ayu Plays a Very Important Role in Expanding the Sales of Jamu Nyonya Meneer.*

This thesis described the strategy of promoting a product through advertising. Charles explained the hurdles he had to overcome in detail before his thoughts and inspirations were accepted because in the beginning they had appeared strange and too extreme.

His patience and hard work proved to be worthwhile. On his return to Indonesia he was ready to apply the methods and theories he had studied.

Another campaign was elevating the prestige of jamu in general. Through mass media advertisements, customers would get to know Nyonya Meneer's products and the company itself. It would not bring a fast profit, but would establish a long-term image for the company. Customers began to put more trust in traditional remedies, and sales continued to grow across the company's entire product line.

By the mid-1980s, Nyonya Meneer's market share, sales and profits were at record highs. However, the breakthroughs in distribution and marketing were beginning to show weaknesses in the management structure. The costs of running the advertising campaigns drew heavy criticism from parts of the family, and the company was about to face its first real management crisis.

The proverbial straw that broke the camel's back was a product called Vitasae. Vitasae was, unbelievably, an alcoholic sport drink made from fermented rice (*tape ketan*). The alcohol level was 5%, and market research revealed that consumers didn't mind as it was all-natural.

Before rolling out a national campaign, Charles wanted to introduce the product in East Java. He hired Linda Saputra, the movie star, to appear in a TV advertisement on the state-owned TVRI channel, combined with newspaper and magazine advertisements. The sales were so strong that the production facility in Semarang couldn't keep up with the demand. The advertising costs were very high as well, and the other family members in the company's management began to question his marketing tactics.

Before his planned national campaign for Vitasae, Charles was informed that production had to stop because the fermentation process of the rice made the female workers unable to menstruate. Feeling this was just an excuse to bring his national roll out campaign to a halt, the looming management crisis was brought out into the open in 1984 with two clear sides emerged: Hans Pangemanan as

President Director and Nonie Saerang as Commissioner supported Charles's marketing campaigns, while Marie and Lucie as the other Commissioners disapproved at the expenditures and wanted a more active role in the management of the company.

Marie told Charles if there would be a conflict in the management, then she, as production director, would simply halt production. Charles then approached Nonie and asked if she was able to make the different kinds of jamu in a separate factory. Nonie said she could, and it would take four months to get an off-site factory prepared. With this information, Charles put his plan in motion. He contacted all of his agents and got them to buy enough stock of Nyonya Meneer's jamu to last for six months. Most agents agreed, but several did not. For those areas where the agents did not agree to participate in the plan, Charles simply appointed new ones. One of the problems was the Surabaya agent was Lucie's son, Hengky. Around this time Hengky was having territorial disputes with the agent in Malang. Since Charles could not reveal his plan to Hengky, he gave the instruction to the Malang agent to infiltrate the Surabaya region.

Keeping her promise, Marie began to develop shortages of certain products to prove her power and value in the company. Charles and Hans Pangemanan secretly met with Sudomo, the Minister of Manpower, and told him of the management problems in the company and the only way to fix them would be if he would step in. Sudomo recognized the thousands of households that were dependent on the company, and agreed to mediate with the shareholders.

After months of mediation, a compromise was reached. Hans Pangemanan would stay as President Director, and Marie's son, Fitzsimons Kalalo, would be appointed his deputy. Unfortunately, this compromised was flawed from the start. Both Hans and Fitzsimons could not agree on anything and the conflict between the two groups grew deeper and deeper. Decisions were made by both directors that contradicted each other, and the company's thousands of employees were stuck in the middle and forced to choose a side.

The infighting was not just verbal either: in January 1985, a fight broke out between an employee loyal to Fitzsimons and the head of security who was loyal to Hans. The situation had reached a tipping point and both sides knew change had to come – and it had to come fast.

As the management was deadlocked, the company's production plummeted and 1300 workers were laid off. Shocked at the social ramifications of this management conflict, Sudomo was forced to step in again to find a more permanent solution.

On November 28, 1985, Sudomo organized a mediation meeting between the two groups in Jakarta. Present were all the five shareholders: Hans, Nonie, Lucie, Marie and Charles, as well as high-ranking members of the Ministry of Manpower as witnesses. Many options were explored, but the differences in management were too great and the only solution would be for one party to buy the other party out. Marie and Lucie agreed to sell their 40% block of shares to Hans, Nonie, and Charles, and all decided the next step would be to appraise their shares and determine a purchase price.

Almost immediately, further problems developed. Both sides appointed an appraiser for the shares and unsurprisingly both groups were given different values. Sudomo stepped in again and organized a second meeting on December 2. The essence of the appraisal problem was determining a proper value of the company's fixed assets, and since production was frozen the value of the company was declining on a daily basis.

With the company effectively closed during this conflict, workers in Semarang began to protest. Sudomo immediately boarded a plane for Semarang and held numerous discussions with the different divisions, explained the company's management position and most importantly, promised all the workers would be paid in full and on time.

Over three months later, on March 20, 1986, all parties finally agreed on a price for the 40% block of shares. Twenty-five members of the family showed up, and the handover ceremony was officiated by Sudomo himself. Lucie and Marie were officially bought out by Hans, Nonie, and Charles. Hans would stay on as the company's President Director, Charles as the Marketing Director, and Nonie as Commissioner. The three immediately got to work to fix the internal problems created by the shareholders conflict, and an advertising campaign was launched to announce to the nation that PT Nyonya Meneer was back in business.

Nyonya Meneer's Jamu Museum, factory, and assembly building at
Jalan Kaligawe, Semarang (1988).

The interior of Nyonya Meneer's Jamu Museum,
Indonesia's and the world's first museum dedicated to jamu, inaugurated 18 January 1984.

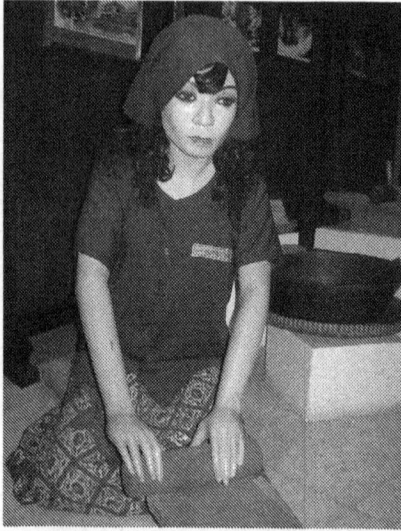

A mannequin inside the Jamu Museum.
It demonstrates one of the traditional ways to make jamu, called "pemipisan,"
where dried herbs and plants are mixed with water and smoothened to create a thick paste.
Then, the paste is dried to make tablets or pills. Today, specified machines replace this manual process.

Mannequins inside the Jamu Museum showing another way of producing jamu
called "penumbukan," where plants with tough layers are crushed with a stick called "alu"
and mixed with other herbs in an oversized bowl called "lesung" to create fine granules.
Usually this process is done by more than one person simultaneously. Advanced machines are now
being used to replace this traditional process.

59

Newspapers' coverage of the first management crisis in Nyonya Meneer.

SUARA MERDEKA ● JUMAT, 21 MARET 1986

Penyelesaian Pembayaran Saham Jamu "Nyonya Meneer" Dilakukan di Depan Menaker

PENYELESAIAN pembayaran saham perusahaan jamu Nyonya Meneer kepada pihak kedua yang sepakat menjual sahamnya sebanyak 40 persen kepada pihak pertama yang memiliki saham 60 persen, Rabu petang dilaksanakan di ruang kerja Menteri Tenaga Kerja Sudomo di Depnaker Jakarta. Pelaksanaan pembayaran itu dilakukan di depan notaris yang disetujui oleh kedua belah pihak dalam keluarga pengelola perusahaan jamu yang tadinya bersengketa itu dengan disaksikan Menaker Sudomo.

Demikian sumber berita yang diperoleh Suara Merdeka dari kalangan depnaker. Rombongan keluarga PT Jamu Nyonya Meneer yang terdiri sekitar 25 orang berikut notaris dan pegawai sekretariat datang ke Depnaker jam 11.30 dan diterima Menaker Sudomo jam 12.00. Pertemuan tersebut tertutup untuk pers, karena masih ada beberapa masalah yang harus diselesaikan.

Kedua belah pihak yang tadinya bersengketa itu diterima secara terpisah, kemudian kedua pihak tadi masing-masing berunding di tempat yang berlainan. Hasil perundingan itu selanjutnya dibawa ke pertemuan bersama, untuk ditandatangani.

Menurut sumber berita itu, pertemuan tersebut tidak begitu mulus, karena masih ada perincian yang kurang jelas mengenai naskah penjualan saham, sebelum disahkan oleh notaris. Akhirnya pada pukul 16.30 WIB Rabu petang, pertemuan mereka selesai dan notaris mengesahkan penjualan saham tersebut kepada pihak yang sekarang sepenuhnya mengelola perusahaan jamu itu.

Batas Waktu

Menurut sumber berita yang diperoleh Suara Merdeka itu sejak disepakatinya penyelesaian persengketaan di PT Jamu Nyonya Meneer awal Februari lalu, pembayaran saham sebanyak 40 persen akan dilakukan kepada pihak yang berhak, selambat lambat-

nya tanggal 20 Maret 1986. Tetapi sampai waktu yang ditentukan kemarin ternyata masih terjadi sedikit kesulitan dalam perincian pembayarannya, khususnya yang menyangkut klos-klos jamu itu yang bertebaran di banyak tempat.

Belum diperoleh keterangan hasil sebenarnya pertemuan keluarga besar PT Jamu Nyonya Meneer di depnaker itu. Para wartawan gagal mendapat keterangan dari Menaker Sudomo Rabu malam lalu seusai ceramah Pangab/Pangkopkamtib Jenderal LB Moerdani, karena malam itu juga menaker harus berangkat ke Bandung untuk suatu acara Kamis pagi kemarin. (jrt).

"Transfer of Shares Witnessed by Minister of Manpower" (Suara Merdeka, 1986).

BUANA MINGGU, Minggu Kliwon, 13 April 1986

Syukuran tuntasnya kemelut PT Nyonya Meneer

Semarang,
(Buana Minggu)

Sistem pengobatan tradisional memegang peranan penting dalam masyarakat Indonesia yang merupakan tolok ukur keberhasilan program pembangunan kesehatan.

Peran penting pengobatan tradisional ini terutama dalam upaya mengatasi penyakit umum seperti sebabis melahirkan, sakit maag, sariawan dan masuk angin. Pada jenis penyakit terakhir ini, pengobatan secara tradisional bisa membantu para petugas kesehatan dan penderita yang bersangkutan dalam memberikan pertolongan pertama, yaitu dengan minum Jamu Singkit Angin misalnya. Jamu Singkit Angin ini untuk mengobati semua gejala masuk angin seperti perut kembung, mual, kepala pusing dan lain sebagainya.

Bumi Indonesia yang kaya akan tanaman obat-an telah mengenal ramuan tradisional sejak dulu kala. Sebagian besar dari masyarakat Indonesia secara teratur minum jamu tradisional. Mereka mulai mencari obat yang terbuat dari alam, yang tidak mengandung efek sampingan. Bahkan masyarakat luar negeri seperti Jepang, Amerika, Australia dan Eropa pun mulai menggandrungi pengobatan tradisional Indonesia.

Kalau kita perhatikan, daerah Jawa Tengah merupakan pusat industri jamu. Banyak pabrik jamu muncul dari Jawa Tengah ini. Industri jamu yang tergolong tua di Jawa Tengah diantaranya Jamu Nyonya Meneer. Pabrik jamu ini yang beberapa waktu

lalu terpaksa meliburkan karyawannya 1,5 bulan dengan mendapat gaji penuh, kini semuanya telah berjalan lancar sebagaimana mestinya, karena permasalahan kemelut keluarga yang dialami Nyonya Meneer telah selesai tuntas.

Penyelesaian kemelut Nyonya Meneer tersebut disaksikan Menteri Tenaga Kerja Sudomo, dan disaksikan dengan akte notaris di Jakarta pekan lalu. Saat ini yang sangat menggembirakan bagi perusahaan adalah: adanya kenyataan bahwa walau terhenti berproduksi selama 1,5 bulan, namun simpati dan minat konsumen terhadap jamu Nyonya Meneer tetap seperti semula. Setelah penyelesaian kemelut tersebut dan produksi jamu telah berjalan normal kembali, maka

Suasana syukuran di Perusahaan Jamu PT Nyonya Meneer

pada hari Minggu 30 Maret y.l. diadakan syukuran bersama keluarga besar PT Nyonya Meneer dan karabat PT. Acara syukuran dilaksanakan dalam satu jamuan, untuk karyawan bagian staf dan karabat kerja di Ramayana Room Hotel Patrajasa Semarang.

PT Nyonya Meneer yang sudah berusia 67 tahun ini memproduksi 120 macam jamu untuk perawatan kesehatan/kecantikan. Mengenai promosi dan kuantitasnya sekaligus dilanjutkan seperti semula.

"Celebrating the End of Conflicts in Nyonya Meneer" (Buana Minggu, 1986).

"Surabaya Post" Rabu, 4 Juni 1986

DUA pewaris yang dikenal sebagai kelompok peramu jamu Ny. Meneer Semarang, membangun perusahaan jamu baru. Sebelah kiri, Ny. Lucy Saerang (putri ketiga) dan Ny. Marie Kalalo (putri keempat).

Peramu Jamu "Nyonya Meneer" Buka Pabrik Baru di Rungkut

SURABAYA: Bekas kelompok peramu jamu "Nyonya Meneer" yang juga putra mendiang Ny. Meneer sendiri, Ny. Lucy Saerang dan Ny. Marie Kalalo, menyatakan tidak mau melibatkan diri lagi, dengan perusahaan jamu Ny Meneer.

"Kami sudah tidak ada kecocokan lagi dengan kelompok manajemen (mayoritas) yang merupakan penegang saham terbesar di Ny. Meneer," kata Ny. Lucy yang didampingi oleh adiknya, Ny. Marie, kemarin di Surabaya. Kemelut antarpemegang saham yang berlarut-larut, memaksa keduanya untuk membuka perusahaan jamu baru

yang bernama "Dua Putri Dewi" berlokasi di Rungkut Industri, Surabaya.

J.L. Saerang, putra dari Ny. Lucy Saerang diberi kedudukan menjadi Presiden Direktur dalam perusahaan jamu baru ini, dan Drs. Pitzsimons Kalalo yang putra dari Ny. Marie Kalalo menjabat Direktur Promosi. Drs. J.G. Kalalo yang putra Ny. Marie Kalalo sebagai Direktur Produksi.

"Mendiang ibu kami asli dari Sidoarjo, dan beliau pernah memberi amanat bahwa keturunannya harus bisa melanjutkan usaha mendirikan jamu," kata Ny. Mario mengenang. Sebenarnya Ny. Meneer hanya mewariskan kepandaiannya meramu jamu pada anak perempuannya saja. "Kami berdua sudah menuruti amanat beliau hanya seorang saudara tertua kami yang perempuan, Ny. Nonnie Saerang tidak menguasai ini, dan memilih membuka penjualan di Jakarta," tambah Ny. Lucy.

DOMINAN

Dalam perusahaan seperti ini,

sebenarnya posisi peramu sangat dominan, tapi keduanya sudah tidak tahu lagi bagaimana jadinya dengan jamu Ny. Meneer sepeninggal mereka. Menurut Ny. Lucy dengan mendirikan perusahaan jamu baru, sudah bisa dikatakan melanjutkan amanat ibunya.

J.L. Saerang sendiri tidak berani tampil untuk mendirikan jamu baru kalau tidak didukung Ny. Lucy dan Ny. Marie yang ahli meramu jamu ini. Merk barunya sengaja tidak diberi embel-embel nama Ny. Meneer. Sebab nama itu sudah menjadi hak paten dari jamu merk Ny. Meneer.

"Kita pakai nama Dua Putri Dewi. Dua putri itu disimbolkan sebagai kedua ibu kami (Ny. Lucy dan Ny. Marie) sedangkan Dewi sendiri diidentikkan dengan Ny. Meneer," katanya. Keduanya 30 Mei intu sudah pamit ke Gubernur Jateng, Ismail, dan menyatakan untuk mendirikan perusahaan jamu baru di Surabaya. Kota ini dipilih untuk menghindari persengketaan dengan Ny. Meneer yang berlokasi di Semarang. (p-2)

Two daughters of Nyonya Meneer, Lucie and Marie, decided to start their own jamu company, Dua Putri Dewi. "Nyonya Meneer's Jamu Producers to Open Their Own Factory in Rungkut" (Surabaya Post, 1986).

An announcement of the transfer of leadership from the late Nyonya Meneer to her eldest, Nonie Saerang, circa 1986. Top: Nonie Saerang. Standing from left to right: Paul Saerang (Nonie's son), Fiona and Gwyneth (Vera Saerang and Hans Ramana's daughters), Linky and Power Pangemanan (sons of Hans Pangemanan). Sitting down, left to right: Hans Pangemanan and Charles Saerang.

Examples of Nyonya Meneer's early advertising campaigns.

One can see the various strategies utilized by the company to make their products popular. Targeting various groups, from teenage girls, husbands and wives, to older folk, the ads often feature attractive graphics and famous models.

Advertisement for Sorga Herbs, a jamu to improve sexual intimacy – later the product was renamed Jamu Tresnasih (1981).

An advertisement featuring Memedi, a popular comedy group sponsored by Nyonya Meneer (1981).

Bedak Dewi Kecantikan, face powder (1980).

Jamu Parem Kocok for muscle pains and better blood circulation (1981).

Jamu Sarang Burung, advertised to increase energy during the Islamic fasting month (1981).

Young actress Cornelia Agatha promoting beauty powder Bedak Remaja Nyonya Meneer (1989).

Ad for Jamu Anggur Sae, which later became
Vitasae, the product that ignited the first
management conflict in the company (1984).

Jamu Gadis Remaja, for teenage girls
who just had their first period (1981).

Ada dua sahabat Chicha Koeswoyo; jamu Gadis Remaja® dan Bedak Remaja®

Chicha... wajahnya segar berseri-seri, membuat bahagia yang melihatnya. Ia telah remaja kini, dan memilih apa yang baik untuknya.

Jamu Gadis Remaja Nyonya Meneer. Untuk Chicha, jamu telah menjadi bagian dari hidupnya sejak kecil. Sejak haid pertama, ia tak lupa minum Jamu Gadis Remaja secara teratur disela hari-harinya yang ceria. Agar tubuh tidak mekar secara berlebihan, tetap singset dan segar.

Bedak Remaja Nyonya Meneer. Satu lagi sahabat Chicha. Selalu dipakainya agar kulit wajah menjadi lembut, segar dan cantik berseri.

Dari dalam tubuh, Jamu Gadis Remaja membantu memancarkan kesegaran remaja. Sedangkan Bedak Remaja membantu dari luar tubuh. Chicha berharap semua rekan remaja juga menggunakannya.

Jamu Nyonya Meneer Semarang, tradisi terbaik untuk merawat kesehatan dan kecantikan.

Kembang Remaja Chicha Koeswoyo : "Jamu Gadis Remaja®dan Bedak Remaja® adalah sahabat Chicha yang sejati"

"Kawan-kawan remaja, sejak haid pertama, Chicha tidak lupa minum Jamu Gadis Remaja secara teratur. Untuk menjaga agar tubuh tetap singset, berisi dan segar.

Nah, itu perawatan dari dalam. Dari luar, Chicha selalu memoles Bedak Remaja agar kulit wajah tetap lembut, segar dan cantik berseri.

Pokoknya begini, deh!

Untuk merawat kesegaran dan kecantikan, Jamu Gadis Remaja dan Bedak Remaja betul-betul sahabat Chicha yang sejati. Sebaiknya, kalian pun menggunakannya"

Jamu Nyonya Meneer Semarang, tradisi terbaik untuk merawat kesehatan dan kecantikan.

Colorful advertisements for Jamu Gadis Remaja featuring teen celebrity Chicha Koeswoyo (1982, 1983).

Kelembutan wajah Ira, dilindungi oleh Neera Nyonya Meneer

Wajah lembut yang ayu. Bebas jerawat, halus
o.empesona. Karena Bedak Jerawat Neera
Nyonya Meneer.

Bedak Jerawat Neera Nyonya Meneer
ramuan khusus untuk mencegah dan
mengobati jerawat.

Melenyapkan noda bekas jerawat, membuat wajah
senantiasa bersih, halus, segar terpelihara.
Bagi Ira, juga Anda, Neera pelindung ceria remaja.

Jamu Nyonya Meneer Semarang, tradisi terbaik untuk merawat kesehatan dan kecantikan

*Advertisement for Bedak Jerawat
Neera powder to treat acne;
the model is Ira Maya Sopha, also a
teen idol (1983).*

Ira Maya Sopha :
" Wajahku lembut, wajahku halus berkat
Bedak Jerawat NEERA NYONYA MENEER."

*Another advertisement for
Bedak Jerawat Neera
featuring Ira Maya Sopha (1985).*

The Evolution of Awet Ayu Advertisements

*One of the first Awet Ayu advertisements, featuring GRA Retno Satuti,
a palace princess of Solo (circa 1980s).*

*Advertisement for Awet Ayu scrubbing
cream (1981).*

*Another example of the early Awet Ayu campaign
(circa 1980).*

To encourage purchase, the company held a lottery for those using Awet Ayu products (1989).

Awet Ayu targets women of all ages.
This ad appeals to both mothers and daughters (1987).

*Actress Diana Pungky
promoting Awet Ayu (1992).*

*Calendar advertisement for
Awet Ayu body lotion (1992).*

*Actress Nia Zulkarnaen
also promoting Awet Ayu (1992).*

Awet Ayu is said to "preserve natural beauty" (1998).

One of the latest ads for Awet Ayu, featuring a palace princess of Solo, the graceful GKR AYU Koes Indriyah (2006).

The first packaging for the product that became Awet Ayu Buste Cream.
In the 1940s, it was called Bustekruiden.

Modern advertisement for Awet Ayu Buste Cream, featuring Ratna Listy, a well-known Indonesian presenter and actress (2003).

Still promoting Buste Cream, targeting women of all ages featuring Femmy Permatasari (presenter and celebrity) and Lili Siswanto (expert on traditional beauty product) (2000).

Article in women's magazine Kartini,
explaining the benefit of Awet Ayu Buste Cream (2002).

One of the most recent ads for Buste Cream (2005).

CHAPTER THREE
THE SECOND CRISIS

WITH THE new management firmly in place and all the conflicts re-solved, the company wasted no time rebuilding its image and develop-ing more innovative products.

One of challenges the company Nyonya Meneer faced in the mid-1980s was ensuring an adequate supply of raw plants and herbs for continuous jamu production. If the prices were not high enough, farmers simply would not plant the medicinal herbs and go back to rice-farming where the price was stable and the demand strong. In the worst case, the skills of planting these herbs could be entirely forgot-ten, thereby setting the entire traditional jamu industry on a course for extinction.

Like most commodities in Indonesia, the trade in medicinal plants and herbs was controlled by brokers. It was also the brokers who controlled the price – not the farmers nor the jamu companies – and therefore they wielded enormous power over the fate of the industry. Also, given the wide range of quality in essential ingredients such as ginger, turmeric, curcuma, anise, fennel, and clove, the prices would fluctuate and make it near impossible for the companies to forecast their raw material expenditures.

Following on his success of working with his distributors as business partners, Charles took the same approach with the farmers. He initiated something called the Plasma Program, which was a series of training seminars for the farmers to show them modern techniques of growing high-quality plants and herbs. He reasoned the higher the quality of the raw material, the higher the price that could be offered and the greater the incentive for the farmers to continue planting the materials his company needed at that time and well into the future.

Charles hired instructors from Gadjah Mada University's School of Agriculture especially to train farmers. After weeks of intense training, the farmers were expected to be able to produce high quality raw material in large quantity. During the initial stages, the company also offered a fixed salary to farmers to maintain enthusiasm in the program.

The Plasma Program was a resounding success. On the company's 70th anniversary in 1989, Nyonya Meneer invited farmers from all over Indonesia to participate in the celebrations. Like the agents and distributors, the farmers now felt that they were business partners with the company and they would look after it like their own.

Looking after farmers and distributions was one thing, but Charles realized he needed to shift some of his attention to his own employees. They have always been treated as part of Nyonya Meneer's extended family since the early days, and indeed several of the active employees were among the first original employees that Nyonya Meneer herself hired. In 1986, the company employed over 1000 workers, and this figure would increase by 50% in the following five years. Charles wanted to close the gap between management and the workers, so the company began giving awards for excellent achievement, organizing staff training programs, and hired special workforce consultants to monitor the workers, listen to their complaints, and devise ways to upgrade their general welfare. This system was a success for both the workers as well as the management. With a renewed sense of belonging and ownership, the employees produced high quality products that could compete in the marketplace. This led to an increase in sales, which led the management to institute even more loyalty and performance bonuses. For a while, it appeared that Nyonya Meneer was firmly back on track to dominate the market for jamu.

With the management problems behind them, Charles began to implement his plan to widen the market for jamu even more. In the late 1980s, there was strong speculation that the growth of the over-the-counter pharmaceutical business would devastate the traditional medicine business. Essentially, jamu is delivered in three forms: powder, pills and capsules. The best-selling form at the time – and continues today – is powder which had a notoriously bitter taste. Nyonya Meneer's chemists got to work on converting all the powders to pill and capsule form and even invented flavors for jamu like chocolate, orange, and strawberry for the emerging children's market.

The innovation did not stop there. In 1989, Nyonya Meneer further diversified their product portfolio by making a range of cosmetics, soap and shampoo, as well as adding a portfolio of products for men. Not all were marketed in the same way or with the same capital commitment – very careful market research was always done to give an indication of which would be the blockbuster products.

The other obvious market for Nyonya Meneer's jamu was international. Historically, jamu was not marketed or sold abroad as no company put the proper budget or manpower behind it. Given Charles's international exposure, he felt that his jamu could compete directly with other country's traditional and over-the-counter medicines. First, though, he had to raise awareness for jamu itself.

While Nyonya Meneer had been a regular fixture at domestic trade fairs, Charles began participating in fairs in Malaysia, Taiwan, the Netherlands, and even was a co-sponsor of the 1986 Asian Games in Seoul, South Korea. Brunei Darussalam became a good market for Nyonya Meneer as well. During an exhibition, the Princess of Brunei, Sri Kayah Mariam, visited their stand and tried Awet Ayu herself. She was very impressed and began a personal campaign to promote jamu around her country.

As President Director since 1985, Hans Pangemanan led the company in a manner similar to his mother. This included living in Semarang, developing strong ties with all the workers, and keeping a control of every aspect of the company. He preferred stability to growth, and this led to constant differences of opinion with his nephew, Charles. Charles became convinced that in order for the company to thrive in the coming new millennium, they would have to have a reorganization of the management structure.

During the annual shareholder meeting in December 1989, Nonie broached the subject of a management reshuffle. She agreed with Charles that the top position should be filled with someone who could lead the company into the 21st century, and she felt the only person that could do that was Charles himself. In the previous ten years, Charles had made great progress in the marketing of Nyonya Meneer, as well as securing a high quality supply of raw materials and training staff to become more efficient. There was a surprising lack of dissent, and the matter was put to an immediate vote. Within one hour of convening the shareholders meeting, Charles was appointed President Director of Nyonya Meneer and the company officially entered into its third generation of management.

For the next ten months, Charles completely restructured and streamlined the executive management and the human resources department. The reporting lines were untangled and job descriptions were made transparent. Just when the restructuring was complete, Hans informed Charles that his appointment as President Director the previous December was illegal and Hans would resume operational control of the company.

In October 1990, Hans brought evidence that there was a procedural error in the signing of the President Director appointment resolution. He claimed that as Gwyneth, Charles's sister, had taken Australian citizenship, she was forbidden to vote and therefore the entire resolution was null and void.

Charles knew it didn't matter if one of the commissioners was a foreign national or not. Angry, he called for an extraordinary meeting of the shareholders to resolve this issue once and for all. The programs that he implemented not long ago were just beginning to bear fruit, and he knew that without him at the helm the future of the entire company was at risk.

The meeting was held in Jakarta on December 14, 1990. In contrast to the meeting a year prior, this one did not run smoothly. Over the past year Hans divided his shares amongst his three children, and all demanded to have a seat at the table. Under the company's constitution, each shareholder would have a maximum of 6 votes. Previously Hans had only six votes for his 67 shares, but since he divided his shares amongst his children, his side now had 18 votes.

Chaos reigned. Charles protested that the share transfer was not legal, and Hans produced a notarial deed that specified the division of Hans's shares. While this appeared to be legal, the new shareholders were not listed in the official share registry, and therefore should be excluded from the meeting. Both sides were unwilling to compromise, and Charles decided to leave the meeting.

After an hour, all sides reconvened in the conference room. To complicate matters further, Nonie declared that all of Hans's duties would be immediately suspended and temporarily be assigned to the President Commissioner. While technically Nonie was able to make this declaration under the company's bylaws, Hans immediately rejected it and threatened to go public with the entire story of the turmoil at Nyonya Meneer.

Nonie held firm. She maintained the initial reason for Hans's suspension was that he failed to report the company's financial statements to the Board of Commissioners during his entire tenure as President Director from 1985 to 1990. The shareholders agreed that no one would be able to settle the current deadlock and that the meeting would reconvene one month later to decide Hans's fate.

On January 12, 1991 the meeting was reassembled at the Sahid Jaya Hotel in Jakarta. The main reason for this meeting would be for Hans to explain why he didn't report any financial statements during this tenure, but Hans refused to attend. He claimed that on the invitation he was only listed as a shareholder and not as the suspended President Director. Instead, he sent his attorney as his proxy.

As in the December meeting, two of Hans's children forced their way into the boardroom, claiming they, as shareholders, had every right to be there. Their names, however, were still absent from the share registry and they were quickly escorted out of the room.

Nonie, as President Commissioner, expressed reservations about continuing the meeting without Hans present. The intention of this meeting was to decide who would lead the company, and she felt without Hans's presence the decisions would not be legally binding in a court of law. Hans's lawyer rejected the argument and demanded the meeting to continue. Their request was denied and Hans's lawyer and paralegals finally left the room.

The remaining shareholders decided that this had gone too far. They had shown good will giving Hans a chance to defend himself and were rebuffed. Sensing that this might never reach a resolution, the shareholders changed their earlier stance and called for a vote and again the results were unanimous: Hans Pangemanan was dismissed from the President Director position effective December 14, 1990; Charles was appointed as the new President Director; Nonie Saerang resigned from the Board of Commissioners; and Vera Saerang and Nonie's husband, Oke Saerang, would be appointed the new Commissioners.

As expected, Hans rejected this decision. He argued that the meetings and the decision made were not legal as he was not given the opportunity to defend himself. Three days after the vote to dismiss him, he sued the six shareholders (his sister, sister-in-law and four nephews) in a Semarang Court on January 15, 1991, claiming that the January 12 meeting was illegal. For good measure, he sued the attending Notary Public, R. Santoso, as well for dereliction of duty. He demanded that the January 12 meeting be declared illegal, confiscation of all properties and land owned by the company, and damages in the amount of Rp 5 billion (about US$2.5 million at the time).

While the court was processing these accusations, the company continued to have two president directors, and neither would give up their position. Hans refused to vacate the office of the President Director, seized corporate and shareholder documents, and continued to use company letterhead and sign agreements as President Director. Hans's sons, Finance Director Power Pangemanan and the Head of the Delivery Bureau, Linky Pangemanan, refused to follow any instruction issued by Charles and claimed loyalty to their father as President Director. Charles decided to act and on February 9, 1991 the Board of Commissioners voted to relieve Hans's children from their positions for insubordination.

But that wasn't enough. Step by step, Charles tried to reclaim his position at the helm of the company by enlisting support from the Mayor of Semarang and the Chief Justice of Semarang's Civil Court. With these two powerful men on his side, Charles felt confident to attempt to go back to work on February 11. The first thing he did was replacing all the locks. Unfortunately, Hans showed up the next day and had all of them changed back.

Sensing the potential devastating impact this feud could have on the company's employees, the Mayor of Semarang, Soetrisno Soeharto, called for a sit-down with Charles and Hans. The mayor initiated a meeting for both parties in his official residence in Manyaran. A truce was called and five agreements were made: First, the President Director's office would be left vacant until there was a decision from the court; second, the President Director's office would be locked and guarded by the police; third, Hans and Charles would temporarily accept the position of Vice President; fourth, their job descriptions would be determined later on the next meeting; and fifth, the Mayor would explain the current situation to all of the company's employees.

Unfortunately, these agreements only lasted five days. Hans entered the offices and demanded to be let into the President Director's office to get some personal documents. Once he convinced the police to let him in, he refused to leave. Mayor Soetrisno, sensing a further escalation of the conflict, asked the Army Commander of Semarang to supervise the area and prevent any clashes with people loyal to Charles.

With Hans still occupying the offices of the President Director, Charles was nearing his wit's end. He had his attorney bring a criminal case against Hans for illegal occupation of private property. Once this case was filed, regional newspapers took notice and Nyonya Meneer's internal conflict was spread wide in the open.

Hans's original lawsuit against the six shareholders went to trial on March 5, 1991. During the opening procedures, Judge Binti urged all parties to reconcile. Even the Governor of Central Java, HM Ismail, tried to intervene and negotiate a compromise where there would not be a clear winner and loser. All parties soundly rejected this advice and the case went to trial.

While the case was in progress, the workers of Nyonya Meneer were quickly getting out of control due to the management vacuum. Charles enlisted support from the Mayor, the Military District Commander and the Chief of Police, and on April 25, 1991 he was escorted to the corporate offices through a sea of supporters of Hans. While there was a clash between police and the workers, it was quickly brought under control. The next day, realizing how dire the situation was, Mayor Soetrisno, Army Lieutenant Commander Ari Soedibyo, Chief of Police H. Gunawan spoke with all the gathered employees and explained what was happening to the management of their company. Mayor Soetrisno told the workers to stay calm and work as usual. The mayor then praised Charles because he had shown his professionalism throughout the entire management conflict. They seemed to quell the workers' immediate fears, but the tension was still running high.

The dispute between Hans and Charles was still continuing in court and now a new problem appeared: worker unrest. After the clash with the police on April 25, 34 employees were suspended. The following week the 34 suspended employees along with a hundred sympathizers gathered at Hans's house for an evening of "solidarity." Hans provided food and drink while they chanted:

Nyonya Meneer siapa yang punya? (Who owns Nyonya Meneer?)
Yang punya Pak Hans saja (The owner is only Mr. Hans)
Bagaimana nasib buruhnya? (How's the workers' welfare?)
Buruhnya tetap jaya (They live happily always)

As Nyonya Meneer was one of the largest and most distinguished companies in Central Java, the local press followed the case closely and the conflict was a fixture on most newspapers front page. Some rumor, some fact, the story of the conflict at Nyonya Meneer was a constant topic of discussions in the business circles all over Indonesia. The situation got so heated that Governor Ismail decided to take control of the mediation himself.

On June 14, the governor invited Hans and Charles to meet in his official residence. The governor suggested two points to end the conflict: 1. Charles steps down from the position of President Director and instead becomes President Commissioner, and 2. All the family members on the Board of Directors should be replaced with professional managers. Charles respectfully replied that he would consider these two suggestions, but on the condition that all the shareholders voted on it in an extraordinary shareholders meeting. With the ultimate Javanese wisdom, the governor understood this as an agreement and led Hans and Charles to meet the journalists outside his residence for a photo opportunity of the two shaking hands.

The next day, the newspapers published reports stating, "Nyonya Meneer's Conflict is Over," "Charles and Hans Reconcile," and "Conflict in Nyonya Meneer Ends Peacefully." Governor Ismail explained to the reports that a reconciliation agreement would be signed in the morning and submitted to the court. The next day, however, Charles didn't show up to sign the agreement as he stated he had to wait for the shareholder meeting before he agreed to anything. With no agreement in place, the conflict and trial continued.

On August 15, 1991, the judge handed down their verdict. The case by Hans was considered legally weak and was thrown out. The judge declared the legitimate share composition as follows: 67 shares for Nonie Saerang, 15 shares for Charles Saerang, 36 shares for Vera Saerang, 8 shares for Gwyneth and Fiona each, and 67 shares for Hans Pangemanan. Charles was to resume his role as President Director effective immediately.

Upon hearing the verdict, Hans Pangemanan immediately filed an appeal with the High Court of Central Java. On December 22, 1991, after reviewing the case, Justice Boris Harahap upheld the lower court's decision and reiterated Charles was the legal President Director of Nyonya Meneer. Not giving up, Hans filed an appeal with the Supreme Court and on August 31, 1993, the Supreme Court announced they refused to hear the appeal and upheld both previous verdicts. The battle for leadership of Nyonya Meneer was officially over.

Without a role in the operations of Nyonya Meneer, Hans decided to sell his shares to Charles and Nonie. The mediation was led by John Himawan, Lucie Saerang's son, and the parties agreed on a price in less than three months. The share transfer agreement was signed on June 1, 1994 in the law offices of Gani Djemat in Jakarta, and the physical share release was done on June 9, 1994 at the Graha Santika Hotel in

Semarang, witnessed by Mayor Soetrisno. It was an emotional event – as if all of the problems and conflicts during the past four years were finally over, and while they were not business partners any more, they could resume their family relationship. At the end of the ceremony, Hans and Charles hugged each other while the onlookers' eyes filled with tears. PT Nyonya Meneer was now legally owned by two of the founder's heirs: her eldest daughter, Nonie, and her grandson, Charles.

SEKITAR KEMELUT DI TUBUH "NYONYA MENEER"

Akibat Manajemen Tradisional

Kemelut yang kini sedang melanda perusahaan jamu "Nyonya Meneer" Semarang, cukup menarik untuk disimak. Namun yang terpenting, kita semua menyayangkan bila kemelut tersebut sampai berkepanjangan, sehingga akan mengganggu eksistensi perusahaan jamu tradisional tersebut. Untuk melihat berbagai kemungkinan berkaitan dengan kasus tersebut, berikut analisis Direktur Penelitian dan Pengembangan Manajemen Fakultas Ekonomi UGM, Drs Hiedjarachman Ranupandojo SE, yang disampaikan melalui wartawan KR, Achmad Busyairi. (Red)

KASUS itu pada dasarnya muncul akibat prosedur yang berkait dengan kepemimpinan di perusahaan itu tak dipenuhi. Pimpinannya mengambil jalan sendiri-sendiri. Dari sini, hubungan antar direksi kurang berjalan mulus. Bersamaan dengan itu sifat perseorangan atau individu yang biasanya digunakan dalam perusahaan keluarga telah dibawa masuk ke perusahaan yang telah berbadan hukum. Sifat konvensional diterapkan di model manajemen modern tentu akan menimbulkan benturan.

Tampak pula dalam perusahaan itu mengalami kegagalan komunikasi. Ketegangan-ketegangan psikologis cepat muncul. Lalu, keadaan ini membuat prosedur yang disepakati bersama gampang dilanggkahi.

Dalam manejemen ada dua versi perusahaan yakni perseorangan dan badan hukum. Perusahaan perseorangan manajemen yang dipakai berdasarkan kepercayaan. Keputusan yang dipakai kerap tak melalui kesepakatan. Komonikasi dan prosedur yang dipakai informal. Sementara perusahaan yang berbentuk badan hukum, tidak sekadar kepercayaan melainkan ada delegasi yang sangat diperhitungkan sesuai dengan tugas dan fungsinya demi menggerakkan dan memajukan perusahaan.

Apa yang tampak dalam kasus di perusahaan jamu itu ada fenomena yang mengarah pada transformasi dari manajemen konvensional ke manajemen ilmiah rasional. Dalam kondisi yang demikian ada proses perubahan sikap dari para pengelola perusahaan. Ada benturan nilai-nilai dan pola-pola lama dengan yang baru. Bahkan juga bisa muncul konflik.

Konflik kepemimpinan dalam perusahaan memang bisa terjadi di mana-mana. Di negara maju juga begitu. Untuk itu perlu adanya manajemen konflik. Tujuannya, agar konflik bisa diperpendek waktunya dan bisa diarahkan menjadi positif. Strategi sangat memegang peranan untuk mengatasi konflik intern itu. Namun bila konflik itu berkepanjangan dan tak diarahkan malah berbahaya. Apalagi terus meluas ke semua lapisan tentu bisa membikin kacau dan sangat berpengaruh negatif

pada produktivitas karyawan. Konflik yang berkepanjangan itu pemborosan membuang energi.

Bagaimana agar perusahaan tetap solid dan kalau pun ada konflik bisa memblikin kemajuan? Menurut pendapat saya banyak faktor yang mempengaruhi. Tapi secara umum yang saya amati, masih banyak perusahaan yang belum menerapkan manajemen ilmiah secara utuh. Manajemen yang dipakai masih model lama dengan kepercayaan yang tak realistis. Pendek kata, perusahaan kalau ingin tetap solid dalam waktu yang panjang perlu menata sistem manajemen yang rasional. Dengan cara ini memang banyak tantangan, tapi tantangan itu toh akan membawa kemajuan terutama dalam menghadapi persaingan yang terbuka seperti sekarang.

Saat ini perusahaan yang maju menunjukkan keputusan bersama, waktu yang cepat dengan menggunakan biaya yang minimal. Biaya yang digunakan secara rasional, jelas sasaran penggunaannya untuk menunjang kemajuan perusahaan. Ketiga, membikin kualitas maksimal baik menyangkut produk, pelayanan maupun sumberdaya manusia yang mengelolanya. Keempat, dengan usaha sekecil mungkin, tapi mengarilkan sesuatu yang banyak. Usaha kecil yang dimaksud baik fisik, pikiran maupun mental. Kelima, waktu yang dibutuhkan untuk menata melalih training demi kemajuan perusahaan pendek.

Dalam pengamatan saya konflik-konflik dalam perusahaan banyak yang berkait dengan lima hal itu. Persoalannya, tergantung bagaimana mengelola dan mengarahkan konsep itu secara rinci dan dioperasionalkan dalam perusahaan.

Satu hal lagi yang patut dicatat dalam kasus "Nyonya Meneer" adalah masuknya Walikota dan Muspida Semarang serta upaya hukum yang akan ditempuh.

Saya melihat, campur tangan walikota itu baik. Sebab, konflik itu sudah rumit. Tentu saja sebatas sebagai penengah.

Upaya hukum tentu saja sebagai cara terakhir. Dan ini sangat disayangkan. Jika sebelumnya ada landasan pada kesepakatan bersama dan aturan-aturan perusahaan tentu tak perlu konflik itu terjadi. Saya sarankan, semua pihak berlapang dada. Selesaikan dengan musyawarah. Ingat, banyak karyawan yang cemas melihat konflik itu.

An article criticizing the company's traditional management and encouraging a change to a modern structure (Kedaulatan Rakyat, 1991).

PENGARAHAN PAK WALI: Dengan sikap kebapakan, Wali Kota Semarang, Soetrisno Soeharto tengah memberikan pengarahan kepada sejumlah besar karyawan PT Nyonya Meneer di pabrik perusahaan jamu tersebut di Jl Raden Patah Semarang, Kamis kemarin. Pengarahan Pak Wali itu sebagai salah satu upaya menenangkan kericuhan yang melanda perusahaan tersebut akhir - akhir ini. (Foto: Suara Merdeka / Djoko Badono)

Mayor of Semarang, Soetrisno Soeharto, addressed the factory workers of Nyonya Meneer, asking them to remain calm despite conflicts in the company's management between Charles Saerang and Hans Pangemanan (Suara Merdeka, 1991).

Kemelut 'Nyonya Meneer' ditangani Gubernur Ismail

Semarang, (Wawasan)

Kemelut berlarut-larut yang menimpa perusahaan jamu tradisional PT Nyonya Meneer Semarang ini ditangani oleh Gubernur H Muhammad Ismail. Dalam menangani kasus itu diupayakan melalui jalan alternatif pemecahan. Upaya itu akan ditawarkan kepada pihak-pihak yang bersengketa masing-masing kelompok Charles Ong dan kelompok Hans Pangemanan.

Kepastian itu diungkapkan oleh gubernur kepada wartawan seusai acara silaturrahmi dan berbuka puasa bersama Muspida Tingkat I dengan para ulama se-Jateng di lantai I gedung Satwilda Jalan Pahlawan Semarang, Sabtu malam lalu.

Dengan turuntangannya gubernur, berarti upaya damai yang telah diprakarsai oleh Walikota Sutrisno Soeharto gagal. Dalam pengertian kedua kelompok yang bersengketa tetap belum bisa menerima prakarsa damai yang diupayakan oleh Walikota. Gubernur sendiri pernah mengatakan bahwa dirinya siap mengambilalih penanganan masalahnya apabila walikota tidak berhasil mengatasinya.

Menyinggung alternatif upaya damainya, Gubernur mengemukakan, pertama semua keturunan Nyonya Meneer harus keluar dari operasional perusahaan. Kedua, selanjutnya operasionalisasi perusahaan ditangani orang lain yang tidak memiliki hubungan kekeluargaan. Dan ketiga perlu segera ditempuh penyempurnaan Anggaran dasar/Anggaran Rumah Tangga (AD/ART).

Penyempurnaan AD/ART, kata Ismail perlu dilakukan untuk mencegah jangan sampai muncul lagi benih permusuhan di masa mendatang. Saya sendiri berpendapat, ungkapnya tampaknya ada butir-butir dalam AD/ART yang lemah. "Kelemahan itu akhirnya bisa memancing kemelut,"ujarnya tanpa merinci isi butir yang dikatakan lemah itu.

Ditanya mengenai prakarsa damai yang diajukannya itu, Gubernur mengharapkan agar pihak-pihak yang bersengketa bisa menerimanya. Dan, dia mengaku berharap demikian karena berlarut-larutnya kemelut perlu diselesaikan segera mungkin karena bagaimana pun akan merugikan banyak pihak terutama para karyawan yang harus diperhatikan nasibnya.

Apabila usulannya diterima oleh kelompok Charles Ong dan kelompok Hans Pangemanan, Ismail mengemukakan akan diserahkan kepada pihak pengadilan untuk memutuskannya. Dalam arti ke putusan pengadilan kelak mencerminkan bahwa kemelut di PT Nyonya Meneer bisa diselesaikan secara damai. (L-2.01)

Governor of Central Java, HM Ismail,
intervened to help settle Nyonya Meneer's crisis (Wawasan, 1991).

* Sidang lanjutan kasus Nyonya Meneer siang tadi

Hans Pangemanan tetap mempersoalkan pemecatan dirinya dari jabatan direktur

Hans Pangemanan   Charles Ong

Nyonya Meneer's dispute goes to court. "Hans Pangemanan Still Objects to His Suspension as President Director" (Wawasan, 1991).

154 Karyawan Nyonya Meneer Berharap Dipekerjakan Kembali

Jakarta, Kompas

Sebanyak 154 karyawan Perusahaan Jamu Nyonya Meneer Semarang, masih mengharap bisa dipekerjakan kembali. Hingga saat ini, nasib mereka terkatung-katung tak jelas, bahkan terancam PHK (pemutusan hubungan kerja). Mereka sangat berharap, perselisihan yang terjadi "di atas" antara para pemilik, tidak merugikan karyawan yang tidak tahu apa-apa.

Kuasa hukum 154 karyawan, Budi Riyanto SH dan C Alwi mengemukakan hari Senin di Jakarta, sejauh ini praktis mereka tak masuk kerja, karena dihalangi oleh petugas-petugas keamanan untuk masuk ke lokasi kantor. Kalau ada beberapa yang boleh masuk, mereka harus menggunakan tanda yang bertuliskan *trainee*. "Padahal 154 orang itu semuanya sudah menjadi karyawan tetap bahkan ada yang sudah bekerja 32 tahun," kata Budi yang juga mengaku sebagai salah seorang di antara 154 karyawan yang nasibnya tak jelas.

Ke-154 orang tersebut, ungkapnya, terdiri dari karyawan berbagai tingkatan, ada satpam, pengemudi, operator komputer, karyawan administrasi, manajer, dan lain-lainnya. Sebanyak 34 orang secara resmi mendapat surat skorsing sampai waktu yang tidak ditentukan. Alasan yang dikemukakan dalam surat skorsing itu sama sekali tidak menjelaskan kesalahan dari yang bersangkutan. Namun dalam pertimbangan disebutkan antara lain, perlunya efisiensi dan profesionalisme manajemen perusahaan, serta untuk mengamankan produktivitas perusahaan. "Skorsing kan merupakan salah satu bentuk sanksi, karena itu seharusnya kan ada kesalahan yang dibuat seseorang sehingga ia dijatuhi skorsing," kata Budi maupun Alwi.

Terima uang pinjaman

Meski mereka selama ini tidak bekerja, namun mereka masih menerima uang tiap-tiap bulannya. Uang tersebut menurut Budi sama besar dengan gaji yang mereka terima tiap bulan. Tetapi uang itu tak bisa disebut sebagai gaji karena dalam tanda terima dicantumkan sebagai uang pinjaman.

Menurut Budi, kasus yang dialami 154 karyawan nampaknya erat kaitan dengan terjadinya perselisihan antara para pemilik yang mulai terasa sejak tahun 1986, Hans Pangemanan di satu pihak dengan Charles Ong. Dijelaskan, Hans Pangemanan adalah salah seorang perusahaan jamu cukup terkenal ini — dengan suaminya kedua Nio Tek An. Sedangkan Charles Ong adalah salah seorang cucu Nyonya Meneer dari perkawinannya dengan Ong Bian Wan (suami pertama). "Masalahnya buat kami para karyawan, pertentangan telah mengakibatkan kami menjadi korban," kata Budi.

Menurut dia larangan untuk tidak boleh masuk kerja mulai terjadi tanggal 25 April 1991. Waktu itu karyawan baru saja selesai menikmati cuti lebaran. "Ketika masuk kerja kembali, kami dilarang masuk oleh oknum-oknum berseragam satpam," ujar Budi dan Alwi. Belakangan diketahui, kehadiran oknum-oknum satpam itu atas perintah dari salah satu pimpinan.

Secara resmi, memang belum ada PHK. Namun ke-154 karyawan merasa khawatir, karena gejala ke arah sana sudah mulai kelihatan. Permohonan izin untuk PHK pernah dimintakan secara resmi kepada Kepala Kantor Departemen Tenaga Kerja Kodya Semarang pada bulan Juni 1991.

Sementara Kakanwil Depnaker dalam suratnya kepada pimpinan perusahaan Nyonya Meneer bulan Juli 1991 antara lain menyatakan supaya perusahaan menghindari PHK. Kakanwil juga mengimbau pimpinan untuk menunjukkan rasa tanggung jawab terhadap apa yang pernah mereka ikrarkan di hadapan Gubernur Jateng bahwa tidak akan pernah terjadi PHK.

Untuk itu diharapkan perusahaan mengadakan pembinaan dan menciptakan hubungan yang serasi dan dinamis antara pengusaha dan pekerja. (ret)

154 Karyawan PT. NM Mohon Perhatian Menaker

Jakarta, Juli (BY)

Sebanyak 154 karyawan perusahaan jamu PT Nyonya Meneer, Semarang memohon perhatian Menteri Tenaga Kerja Cosmos Batubara, sehubungan dengan Pemutusan Hubungan Kerja (PHK) yang dilakukan perusahaan tersebut.

Budi Riyanto C. Alwi, yang mewakili 154 karyawan perusahaan itu menjelaskan kepada ANTARA, di Jakarta, Rabu, bahwa PHK yang dilakukan itu bukan karena perusahaan perlu efisiensi atau mengalami kemunduran tetapi semata-mata karena kemelut di antara pimpinan yang saling ingin menguasai perusahaan tersebut.

Dikatakan bahwa Kakanwil Depnaker Jateng Widodo, dalam suratnya tertanggal 20 Juli 1991 yang ditujukan kepada pimpinan perusahaan itu menegaskan, kemelut tersebut berdampak tidak menguntungkan kepada karyawan dan minta untuk tidak melakukan PHK.

Dalam kenyataannya, menurut mereka, perusahaan tetap melakukan PHK, meskipun pada pertemuan dengan Gubernur Jawa Tengah tanggal 14 Juni 1991, pimpinan perusahaan yang diwakili Charles Ong dan Hans Pangemanan berjanji tidak akan melakukan Pemutusan hubungan Kerja.

Dijelaskan, perusahaan untuk menutupi tindakannya itu berlaku tidak jujur, yaitu dengan menghapuskan ke 154 karyawan bersangkutan untuk kembali melamar, tanpa adanya jaminan mereka bisa diterima.

"Jadi perusahaan bisa mengelak dengan mengatakan tidak ada PHK dalam kenyataannya apa yang dilakukan itu pada akhirnya mengarah pada pengeluaran para karyawan," katanya.

Menurut mereka para karyawan ada yang sudah memiliki masa kerja 32 tahun, 28 tahun, 26 tahun dan 19 tahun, yang kesemuanya diharuskan melamar kembali serta tidak dak ada jaminan diterima.

Pemutusan hubungan Kerja atau PHK terhadap ke 154 karyawan tersebut, katanya, diawali dengan tidak membolehkan mereka kembali masuk kerja, yang suratnya di buat pada saat karyawan sedang libur mejelang Hari Raya Idulfitri lalu.

Para karyawan yang tidak bisa bekerja karena ada surat tersebut, dijadikan alasan oleh perusahaan dengan mengatakan mereka tidak bekerja tanpa alasan sehingga merugikan perusahaan.

"Padahal kami tidak bekerja karena ada surat tersebut, tetapi kami tetap berusaha untuk masuk kerja meskipun tidak diperbolehkan masuk ke ruang kerja oleh Satpam yang ditugasi menahan kami," katanya. (Ant)

Top: Upon their suspension, the 154 workers of Nyonya Meneer hoped to be re-employed (Kompas, 1991).

Bottom: "The 154 Suspended Nyonya Meneer Workers Demanded the Attention of the Minister of Manpower" (Berita Yudha, 1991).

88

Power: Bila Perlu sampai Kasasi ke Mahkamah Agung

SEMARANG — Meskipun gugatannya ditolak majelis hakim yang diketuai SM Binti SH, namun sejauh ini pihak Hans Pangemanan belum punya rencana untuk membuka perusahaan jamu lagi seperti yang dilakukan saudaranya di Surabaya. Sebab, pihaknya masih melakukan upaya hukum banding dan bila perlu sampai kasasi ke Mahkamah Agung. Demikian penuturan Power Pengemanan putra Hans. "Konsentrasi saya masih pada persidangan, jadi belum memikirkan buka usaha lagi," katanya lagi.

Putra Hans Pangemanan mengatakan hal itu di kediamannya, sehubungan putusan hakim Pengadilan Negeri yang menolak gugatannya. Putusan Kamis (18/8) lalu itu, menyatakan Charles Ong sebagai Presdir PT Nyonya Meneer dan mengesahkan pemberhentian Hans selaku Presdir.

Begitu pihaknya mendengar putusan, langsung menghubungi pengacaranya Sebyo Handono SH dan Wiryolukito SH untuk minta pengajuan banding. Pendaftaran pernyataan banding, dilakukan sehari setelah putusan. "Begitu Kamis mendengar putusan, Jumat-nya saya minta kepada kuasa hukum untuk mendaftarkan banding di Pengadilan Negeri Semarang," katanya.

Karyawan

Walaupun ada kemungkinan untuk membuka usaha jamu lagi

(Bersambung Hlm XV kol 9)

Power ....

(Sambungan Hlm 1)

gi, namun sejauh ini belum terpikirkan. "Kalau akan berusaha lagi, mungkin di bidang selain jamu," katanya tanpa memberi alasan kenapa dipilih selain jamu.

Sebagai warga negara yang baik, pihaknya akan mematuhi putusan pengadilan dengan ikhlas. Begitu pula dengan perintah hakim untuk mengosongkan ruang direktur. Ini sudah dilakukan sejak ada kemelut perusahaan. "Sudah dikosongkan 4 bulan lalu," katanya.

Putusan tersebut sedikit banyak berpengaruh kepada 154 karyawan yang hingga kini belum menentu nasibnya. Karyawan sebanyak itu, masih berharap untuk dapat masuk kerja lagi. Usaha tersebut sudah dilakukan lewat Depnaker, namun sejauh ini belum ada keputusannya.

Ia akan tetap mengusahakan agar karyawan tidak disangkutpautkan dengan persoalan yang menimpa pihaknya. "Kalau kami tidak begitu resah, namun karyawannya itu yang kasihan," katanya.

Masalah karyawan ini, sudah disampaikan ke Serikat Pekerja Seluruh Indonesia (SPSI) dan Depnaker di Jakarta. Dengan demikian, masalahnya sedang ditangani secara serius. "Kami selalu memikirkan karyawan yang tiap hari berada di rumah," ujarnya. (A.14)

Power Pangemanan, son of Hans Pangemanan: "If Necessary, We Will Appeal to Supreme Court" (Suara Merdeka, 1991).

KASUS PHK 154 KARYAWAN PT NYONYA MENEER
FKP DPR RI Mendesak Menaker Mengabulkan Banding DPP SPSI

SEMARANG (KR) - Fraksi Karya Pembangunan (FKP) DPR RI mendesak Menteri Tenaga Kerja Drs Cosmas Batubara agar mengabulkan permohonan banding DPP SPSI No. 2227/DPP/SPSI/11/1992 tanggal 17 Maret 1992, serta memerintahkan mempekerjakan kembali 154 karyawan PT Nyonya Meneer yang terkena PHK dan memenuhi hak-haknya secara utuh.

The workers gained the attention of the strongest political party in the People's Representative Council (Dewan Perwakilan Rakyat – DPR). The party insisted that the Minister of Manpower grant the workers' appeal (Kedaulatan Rakyat, 1992).

As Charles Saerang gained victory over Hans Pangemanan, the 154 workers who were insubordinate to him were dismissed. In response, Bisnis Indonesia reported that about 5000 companies in East Java had not yet formed a division to take part in the Union of Laborers of Indonesia (Serikat Pekerja Seluruh Indonesia – SPSI), meanwhile SPSI of Central Java demanded that the Minister of Manpower annul the permission to dismiss the workers of Nyonya Meneer.

5.000 Perusahaan di Jatim belum bentuk unit SPSI, dinilai tak bermanfaat

SURABAYA (Bisnis): Sedikitnya 5.000 perusahaan di Jatim hingga kini belum membentuk unit Serikat Pekerja Seluruh Indonesia (SPSI), sementara SPSI Jateng minta kepada Menaker untuk membatalkan (veto) Pemutusan Hubungan Kerja (PHK) 154 karyawan PT Nyonya Meneer (NM).

Menurut Ketua Dewan Pimpinan Daerah (DPD) Jatim, Soedarjanto, perusahaan yang belum membentuk unit SPSI sebanyak itu, berarti lebih besar dari jumlah perusahaan yang sudah merealisasi pendirian unit serikat pekerja.

"Perusahaan yang sudah membentuk unit SPSI kini baru 1.300 atau sekitar 20% dari seluruh perusahaan yang beroperasi di Jatim," ujarnya.

Menurut pengurus SPSI itu berdasarkan laporan yang diterimanya, alasan perusahaan di Jatim enggan membentuk SPSI karena wadah ini dinilai tidak bermanfaat.

"Mereka menilai pembentukan wadah mini bukan merupakan mitra produksi, melainkan menjadi beban perusahaan."

Soedarjanto berterus terang kepada Bisnis bahwa akibat belum banyak didirikannya SPSI di Jatim, maka banyak masalah ketenagakerjaan di provinsi ini tidak dapat diselesaikan secara cepat.

Kedudukan wadah SPSI belakangan ini menghadapi tantangan yang cukup besar. Di Jateng, SPSI dituntut peranannya untuk membantu menyelesaikan kasus PHK di pabrik jamu PT Nyonya Meneer.

"Gubernur Jateng akan meminta Menaker turun tangan untuk meninjau PHK yang terjadi di pabrik jamu PT Nyonya Meneer," kata Ketua DPD SPSI Jateng, Tambah Sudjio.

Kasus ketenagakerjaan yang terjadi di pabrik jamu tersebut dikhawatirkan berjalan cukup lama. Kasus tersebut memuncak baru-baru ini ketika P4P memutuskan surat PHK kepada 154 karyawan PT Nyonya Meneer yang terlibat perselisihan.

Menurut pimpinan SPSI Jateng keputusan yang dikeluarkan oleh P4P itu tidak sesuai dengan etika masyarakat Jateng. "Lantaran itu gubernur Jateng akan mengadakan pertemuan dengan Menteri Tenaga Kerja pada 11 September untuk pembahasan keputusan-keputusan tersebut."

Tambah menghentikan lewat pertemuan kedua pejabat itu dapat memutuskan kasus perselisihan kerja di PT Nyonya Meneer yang telah berjalan cukup lama.

Perselisihan tenaga kerja yang terjadi di Jatim sampai Agustus lalu, menurut catatan pengurus SPSI mencapai 40 kasus. Selain PHK, kasus yang cukup menonjol di wilayah ini adalah pemogokan.

Selain belum membentuk SPSI, kata Ketua SPSI Jatim, kasus perselisihan tenaga kerja di wilayahnya umumnya terjadi karena banyak perusahaan di sini yang belum menerapkan manajemen terbuka.

Untuk mendorong kesadaran agar perusahaan di Jatim mau membentuk SPSI, kata Tambah, organisasinya melancarkan program Tripartit bersama pemerintah dan pengusaha. "Lewat program tersebut kami harapkan dapat membuka wawasan pengusaha mengenai tak dan kewajiban pekerja." (aae/awn)

PEKANBARU (Bisnis): Kantor Pelayanan Pajak (KPP) Tanjungpinang optimis penerimaan pajak untuk anggaran 1991/1992 melampaui target sebesar Rp 58 miliar atau naik sekitar 100% dari penerimaan semula sebesar Rp 93 miliar, kata pejabat di sini, kepada Bisnis, di sini. (ss)

"Tanda Tresna" untuk Mantan Karyawan Nyonya Meneer Dibagi

SEMARANG — Uang tanda tresna dan pesangon untuk 154 mantan karyawan PT "Nyonya Meneer" (NM) yang mengundurkan diri atas kesepakatan bersama, Selasa kemarin mulai dibagikan. Uang tanda tresna sebesar Rp 30 juta dibagikan kepada 154 orang atau Rp 194 ribu/orang. Sedangkan besarnya uang pesangon tergantung masa kerja dan gaji pokok masing-masing.

Pembagiannya dilakukan melalui BPD Jateng kantor kas kodia di kompleks balai kota, diawasi oleh Kakandepnaker Kodia, Drs Roes Sugiat. Hadir pada kesempatan itu antara lain Kabag "Personalia PT "NM", Rewang, Humas Budi Hartini serta Mokhis X dari Panitia Penyelesaian Perkara Perburuhan Daerah (P4D) Jateng.

Kepada sekitar 30 mantan karyawan, Roes Sugiat menyampaikan rasa terima kasihnya atas sikap saling membantu dalam menyelesaikan permasalahan di perusahaan jamu tradisional tersebut. Diingatkan, selain uang tanda tresna, mereka akan menerima surat pengalaman kerja dengan keterangan telah bekerja dengan baik.

"Dalam surat pengalaman kerja itu juga ditulis masa kerja. Surat tersebut sangat diperlukan bagi mantan karyawan untuk mencari pekerjaan di perusahaan lain. Setiap surat pengalaman kerja sudah saya teliti agar tidak ada yang diberi keterangan kurang baik," katanya.

Beberapa mantan karyawan kepada Suara Merdeka mengatakan keberatannya jika disebut di-PHK, sebab mereka tidak melakukan kesalahan. Bahkan, seorang di antara mereka mengaku

menerima pemberitahuan PHK sehari setelah pulang dari tugas promosi ke luar Jawa.

"Sebenarnya kami lebih tepat disebut sebagai 'korban' sengketa antarpimpinan. Jadi kami lebih suka dikatakan mengundurkan diri dan bukan di-PHK," kata Supriyanto, seorang mantan karyawan mewakili rekan-rekannya.

Sempat Waswus

Sejumlah mantan karyawan yang kemarin berkumpul di balai kota sejak pagi, sempat waswas. Sebab, dalam pemberitahuan disebutkan uang tanda tresna akan dibagikan mulai pukul 09.00. Namun hingga pukul 11.30, pembagian belum dimulai.

Tetapi Kakandepnaker Roes Sugiat yang mendampingi mereka berulang kali menegaskan, semua permasalahan dituntaskan hari itu juga. Ternyata keterlambatan itu karena salah informasi. Pihak PT membawa berkas mantan karyawan dan uang ke kantor Depnaker, bukannya ke balai kota. Pembagian akhirnya baru dimulai sekitar pukul 12.00, namun baru untuk 20 orang.

"Setiap orang harus mengambil uang sendiri-sendiri dan jangan diwakilkan," tambah Kakandepnaker.

Di tempat itu, para mantan karyawan juga bisa mengambil SHU koperasi, dan menyelesaikan utang-piutang dengan bekas perusahaan tempat bekerja. Sedangkan barang pribadi yang tertinggal di perusahaan akan diurus kemudian.

Pembagian uang itu—hasil kesepakatan "Patra Jasa" antara LKS Tripartit Pusat yang dipimpin Menaker Cosmas Batubara dengan LKS Tripartit Jateng yang dipimpin Gubernur HM Ismail, belum lama ini—berjalan lancar. Mantan karyawan tampaknya menerima kesepakatan tersebut.

Salah seorang mantan sopir, Supriyanto, yang telah bekerja 9 tahun dan menerima pesangon Rp 1.376 juta mengatakan, puas tidak puas semua itu sudah merupakan kesepakatan. (B7-13)

The distribution of severance pay in the form of "Token of Appreciation" (Tanda Tresna) to the former workers (Suara Merdeka, 1992).

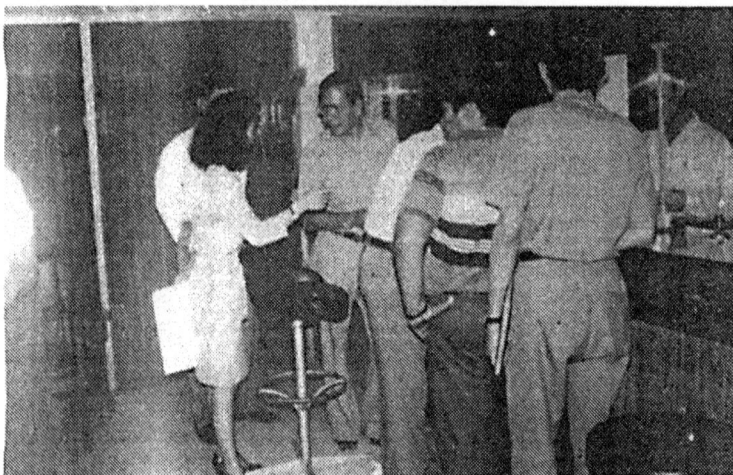

PEMBAGIAN UANG "TANDA TRESNA": Uang "tanda tresna" untuk para mantan karyawan PT Nyonya Meneer yang mengundurkan diri, sejak Selasa kemarin mulai dibagikan. Pembagian dilakukan lewat BPD Jateng Kantor Kas Kota Madia Kompleks Balai Kota Semarang tersebut diawasi oleh Kakandepnaker Kodia Drs Roes Sugiat (menghadap lensa). (Foto: *Suara Merdeka* / B7-34)

Distribution of Tanda Tresna (see previous page).

Setelah Berhasil Terobos Taiwan

200 Produk Nyonya Meneer Menembus Arab Saudi, Juli

SEMARANG
suara indonesia.

PT Nyonya Meneer, sebuah perusahaan jamu tradisional di Semarang akhir Juli mendatang akan malakukan ekspor perdana ke Saudi Arabia, setelah awal tahun ini berhasil menembus Taiwan.

Jika upaya menembus pasaran di negara-negara Timur Tengah nanti berhasil, tidak mustahil sasaran pemasaran ekspor atas Jamu Cap Potret Nyonya Meneer akan beralih kesana, menggeser dominasi negara Taiwan, Malaysia dan Belanda yang selama ini kapasitas impor jamu tradisonal dari sini cukup besar.

"Memorandum Of Understanding (MOU) peluncuran atas produk kami telah ditandatangani bulan lalu dan realisasinya paling lambat akhir bulan Juli tahun ini" kata Presiden Direktur PT Nyonya Meneer Dr. Charles Serang, kemarin di Sema-

rang.

Charles Serang yang juga staf pengajar Fisip jurusan administrasi niaga Universitas Diponegoro (Undip) Semarang tidak bersedia menyebutkan total ekspornya. Hanya menyebutkan bahwa pemasarannya ke Arab Saudi mencatat nilai jualnya mencapai Rp 40 juta/bulan.

Jenis produk yang dipasarkan ke negara petro dollar itu meliputi hampir seluruh jenis produk yang diproduksi industri jamu tradisioanl ini. Hingga kini PT Nyonya Meneer telah memproduksi lebih 200 produk berbentuk ramuan jamu, kapsul dan jenis-

jenis lainnya.

Jika berhasil menembus pasaran di Arab Saudi diharapkan bulan-bulan berikutnya dapat merembes ke negara-negara Timur Tengah lainnya.

"Pasaran Arab Saudi memang sejak dulu telah menjadi incaran kami untuk dijadikan batu loncatan dalam mengembangkan pemasaran ke ka-wasan Timur Tengah dan negara-negara Afrika," kata Charles.

Mengingat para konsumen di kawasan itu saat ini mulai menggemari ramuan-ramuan tradisioanl yang bahannya diambil langsung dari alam dalam upaya merawat kesehatannya yang mulai meninggalkan obat-obatan yang terbuat dari bahan-bahan kimia.

Para konsumen sana mulai menyadari bahwa obat-obatan yang terbuat dari bahan-bahan kimia membawa efek samping yang negatif. "Inilah yang menjadi modal dasar kami hingga pemasaran di kawasan

ini mendapatkan prioritas utama, peluang ini harus dimanfaatkan dengan sebaik-baiknya, mengingat daya beli para konsumen disana cukup tinggi" kata Charles.

Nilai ekspor atas Jamu Nyonya Meneer ke Belanda saat ini mencapai Rp 40 juta/bulan, Malaysia (Rp 70 juta/bulan) dan Hawai (Rp 500 juta/tahun)."Sedangkan nilai ekspor ke Taiwan tiap bulannya mencapai USD 1,5 juta. Sebagian besar produk yang diluncurkan ke Taiwan berupa ramuan tradisional yang diramu dalam bentuk kapsul" katanya.

Untuk memenuhi permintaan konsumen di pasaran internasional yang menginginkan "serba praktis" pihaknya dalam waktu dekat akan meluncurkan ramuan-ramuan tradisioanl yang mempunyai khasiat merawat kesehatan tubuh dalam bentuk kapsul yang bahannya dari satu jenis komoditi seperti jahe, lempuyang, kencur dan lain-lain. (smh)

Thriving despite conflicts: "200 Products of Nyonya Meneer Penetrated the Market of Saudi Arabia"
(Suara Indonesia, 1992).

Nyonya Meneer also actively participates in events to make their jamu more well-known. Here are saleswomen in traditional Javanese costume waiting for customers at the 1985 Jakarta Fair.

A demonstration of the proper way to take jamu, presented at Nyonya Meneer's stand at the 1985 Jakarta Fair.

Nyonya Meneer's stand and saleswomen in traditional Javanese dress at the 1989 Jakarta Fair.

kesinambungan abadi

70 tahun

Semenjak bumi didiami manusia, semua cara mempertahankan diri dilakukan dengan memanfaatkan alam. Dan dengan melestarikan ramuan alami warisan leluhur, **Nyonya Meneer** telah melakukan kesinambungan sejarah.

Didalam era pembangunan, semua hasil bahan baku yang diperoleh diteliti untuk dasar pengembangan proses produksi jamu yang bermutu.

Diterapkannya tehnik pengolahan lahan secara teratur, serta pengolahan bahan baku yang hygienis, ditunjang sarana produksi modern maka dihasilkan produk jamu tradisional yang bermutu tinggi, untuk memenuhi tuntutan masyarakat yang semakin maju.

Semua ini, berawal dari petani sebagai mitra usaha, para pengusaha yang bertanggung jawab, dan bimbingan pemerintah dalam memperoleh hasil yang terbaik untuk membangun bangsa.

.... suatu kesinambungan abadi.

Iklan kelembagaan ini dipersembahkan dalam rangka memperingati 70 tahun P.T. Nyonya Meneer Semarang.

70 Tahun P.T. Nyonya Meneer 1919 – 1989

P.T. NYONYA MENEER

Jamu Nyonya Meneer Semarang, tradisi terbaik untuk merawat kesehatan dan kecantikan

Announcement in national newspaper, Kompas, celebrating Nyonya Meneer's 70th anniversary. Also that year, Charles launched the Plasma Program, which gave training to traditional herbal plants farmers from all over Indonesia.

Charles received the Upakarti Award from Soeharto, former President of Indonesia, for his achievement in supporting the traditional herbal plants farmers (1990).

The opening of the shop Pondok Jamu Nyonya Meneer in Kota Raja, Johor Baru, Malaysia (7 July 1991). This photo shows the company's successful international campaign.

Nyonya Meneer's advertising campaign in the 1990s

Jimas Meneer, containing ginger, honey, milk, and egg for vitality and freshness (1990).

Famous actor Benyamin in a newspaper advertisement for Minyak Singkir Angin, an oil to relieve fatigue and constipation (1994).

Actress Diana Pungky promoting Jamu Neera (1992).

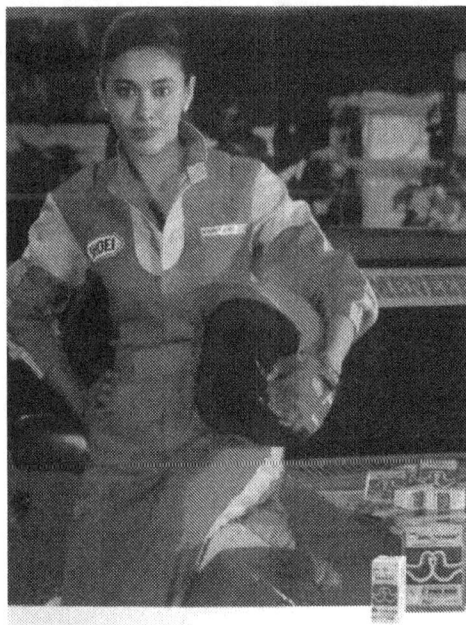

Actress Nia Zulkarnaen, promoting Jamu Tresnasih
to enhance sexual intimacy (1992).

An advertisement in a Malaysian magazine for jamu Galian Singset, a popular slimming product for women in 1998. Targeting 20-something women, Nyonya Meneer hired young models and actresses to promote the product.

Another article in a Malaysian woman's weekly,
this time advertising Jamu Habis Bersalin Istimewa for women after giving birth (1998).

Another article in a Malaysian woman's weekly, explaining the benefits of Jamu Galian Rapet, which enhances female sexual pleasures, here said to promote the happiness of marriage and the family (1998).

In another Malaysian magazine, this article exposes the benefits of Jamu Peputih, claimed to help with yeast infection (1998).

Rahasia Keharmonisan Rumah Tangga

An article and advertisement in an Indonesian business and management magazine,
Kontan, for Jamu Sehat Perkasa, promoted to increase male sexual potency (1998).

Jamu Carang Burung Nyonya Meneer

Suplemen di Saat Puasa

Another article and advertisement in Kontan for Jamu Çarang Burung,
promoted to increase energy and vigor during the fasting month of Ramadan (1998).

Charles Saerang's column in *Obyektif* newspaper,
"Nyonya Meneer's Health and Beauty Consultation," to educate
consumers and promote Nyonya Meneer's products (1999).

KONSULTASI KESEHATAN & KECANTIKAN NYONYA MENEER

KONSULTASI KESEHATAN & KECANTIKAN NYONYA MENEER

CHAPTER FOUR

THE THIRD CRISIS

FROM THE moment the company entered into its third generation in 1989, it was fraught with management problems. What is exceptional though, is despite these problems the company still managed to grow and prosper.

By 1990, there were over 350 independent jamu producers in Indonesia. In order to compete in this environment, Charles implemented several strategies to keep Nyonya Meneer ahead of the pack. He decided that the only way to stave off competition would be to innovate in such a way that the competitors could not easily imitate. He continued with expanding his business lines in cosmetics as well as beefed up his overseas marketing efforts. He invested heavily into research and development to come up with products that were years ahead of his competitors. He assembled a market research team that compiled the most comprehensive database in the industry. Moreover, he formed strategic relationships with clinics, hospitals, universities, and government ministries.

Charles's strategic relationship with Gadjah Mada University was a feat that not only took years to conceive, but was considered unique in the industry that his competitors scrambled to catch up. The basic premise is that jamu can actually improve health as well as cure disease. But the claim needs substantiation – and the only way to prove it is by clinical trials that are internationally certified and accredited.

The clinical test on Rheumaneer, Nyonya Meneer's anti-rheumatism medicine, took four years and cost several hundred thousand dollars – far faster and cheaper than FDA approvals, but considering it was in Indonesia, it was a significant cost in capital and time. The results were a resounding success.

CASE STUDY 2: RHEUMANEER
(see news and images related to Rheumaneer in page 125-26)

The mushrooming of jamu companies in the 1980s had an adverse effect on consumer interests because they did not turn to jamu as their primary medication. Past generations who believed in the benefits of jamu as a cure for illness were happy to rely simply on empirical proofs. The modern generation, however, is not so easy to convince. Unfortunately, until the beginning of the 1990s, no jamu company had proved jamu was a viable alternative to medical products. But in 1992, Nyonya Meneer made a bold and unprecedented step by taking an anti-rheumatic product through a stringent research program, including toxicity and clinical testing, in order to determine scientifically the anti-inflammatory effect of the product.

Most jamu manufacturers employed experts to run quality control tests on products in the company laboratories. However, this exercise was not sufficient to enable them to meet the standard quality requirements. Worse, it had spread the negative idea that jamu companies were not able to authenticate their products clinically. Nevertheless, afraid that the results of scientific tests would fall below their expectations and those of the consumer, other companies were reluctant to put their products through such a risky process.

The medical world had stated openly through the Indonesian Doctors' Association (*Ikatan Dokter Indonesia* – IDI) that they would welcome special jamu remedies on prescription. A prerequisite was passing clinical tests. They felt it would be difficult for them to acknowledge jamu as medicine without tests to discover the benefits, correct dosage, and side effects. This decision was considered absolute and non-negotiable.

An example of a traditional medicine that had passed such testing is the Kina pill. This traditional medicine from India originally occupied the same position as jamu – although it had been accepted as a cure for malaria for generations. Clinical testing was then conducted and it proved Kina could cure malaria. Today Kina is still well-known in the medical world. This illustration showed that clinical testing was indeed a crucial factor in receiving recognition from doctors. At that point, no Indonesian jamu companies had adopted the same approach as the manufacturer of the Kina pill.

Given the lack of evidence, the effectiveness of jamu was still in question. In addition, consumers were growing more and more critical as they now understood how important it was to know what substances went into jamu that was consumed on a daily basis.

At that time, unlike modern pharmaceuticals, jamu packs did not carry an expiration date. Consumers might be uncomfortable to drink jamu without knowing if the product had expired. This defect troubled jamu's image as a traditional remedy for curing illnesses without side effects.

Being one of the biggest jamu companies in Indonesia, Nyonya Meneer was concerned about this reality. Although product manufacture was carefully supervised and quality was being constantly improved, none of their products had reached the stage of clinical testing. This was a major stumbling block that endangered the performance of the jamu business.

To uphold the image of jamu and make it even more popular, Nyonya Meneer seriously prepared to get their products clinically tested. Nyonya Meneer used their well-trained instincts to identify the perfect opportunity. They decided: when jamu products were going through a period of explosive growth, there had to be at least one product officially acknowledged and endorsed by the medical community. At that time, Charles's intuition told him that the period was coming soon. It was time to act, to seize the chance.

Despite being surrounded by problems at work, Charles was determined to proceed with his idea. First, he decided to embark Nyonya Meneer on a total reform, of jamu processing in particular. Instead of depending on techniques handed down from an older generation, from then on jamu would be manufactured using advanced modern technology. Moreover, jamu's excellence and safety must fulfill international standards. The need for this broad vision was urgent. If nothing is done to ameliorate jamu's reputation, it would continue to lag behind modern medicine – it would forever be perceived only as an alternative remedy or dietary supplements rather than a useful system of medication.

It was true, however, that many jamu companies at that time were still reluctant to perform clinical tests on their products. Besides the huge funding that was required, another reason was they assumed that the people would still simply believe in the wisdom of their ancestors who had used these concoctions for centuries. There seemed to be a lack of awareness of or desire to break into the international market, where most people would require scientific testing before using a medicinal product.

Unlike the others though, Nyonya Meneer realized this – and it made them more determined than ever to pass their products as phyto-medicines. They would not rest until they could see their jamu as an official medicine on doctors' prescriptions.

Immediately, Charles sent Nyonya Meneer's special anti-rheumatic jamu to laboratories for testing. He then collected all the data on the ingredients and content to prove the jamu's natural benefits. Charles also fast-tracked this program so that no other traditional medicine manufacturers could outpace him in performing clinical research. There was also a huge pressure of time. ASEAN Free Trade Area (AFTA) had announced that, in order to facilitate globalization, by 2010 scientific tests were required for all natural medicine products that were to be marketed within the area.

In 1991, Nyonya Meneer began work with the Research Center for Traditional Medicine (*Pusat Penelitian Obat Tradisional* – PPOT) at Gadjah Mada University on clinical authentication, using the latest methods and technology.

At first, they faced financial difficulties. The funding required to carry out research on just one product was already exorbitant because there were so many ingredients in every jamu. Each raw material required clinical research and the cost of this would be extortionate. To test just one product a company had to spend hundreds of millions of rupiah – and Nyonya Meneer manufactured 250 products. Therefore, they decided that their jamu would be sent for clinical testing one by one, in order of priority.

Financial problems aside, the tests were ready to be carried out. Nyonya Meneer submitted one product, Rheumaneer, capsules to treat rheumatism. The study was led by Dr. Budiono Santoso from the Clinical Pharmacology Laboratory, Faculty of Medicine, Gadjah Mada University.

The first test conducted was to certify Rheumaneer's anti-inflammatory effect. Male and female mice of 3 to 4 months old, weighing 20 to 25 grams were used as subjects. The mice were given Rheumaneer orally 45.5 mg/kg body weight (equivalent to 350 mg for humans), 182 mg, and 728 mg twice a day. And then 364 mg and 1456 mg once a day. The study found that administering Rheumaneer could reduce inflammation caused by 0.1 ml of formaline, injected below the skin. Administering the jamu twice a day proved more effective than once a day – even with if the accumulated dosage was the same. This test was completed on March 1991.

Next was toxicity tests. Again, male and female mice were used as subjects. Following Weil method (1952), the researchers found that up to the highest dosage that technically could be given orally (LD-50), there were no signs of poisoning and the test animals remained alive. Following WHO method (1975), the researchers discovered that the product, even up to dosage 2500 mg/kg body weight, did not cause any toxic change in the mice. This test was completed July 1992.

Finally, the clinical tests. This study involved 120 patients, male and female, suffering from joint pains, between the ages of 18 to 70 years old. Subjects were randomly divided into three groups. Group A underwent treatment with Rheumaneer, taking two capsules (350 mg each) daily for seven days. Group B acted as positive control, receiving ibuprofen capsules 200-400 mg three times daily for seven days. Group C received multivitamins (two capsules daily for seven days) and acted as negative control.

Assessment of clinical efficacy was done by measuring the degree of joint pains and stiffness before and after treatment, reduction of pains and stiffness, and the overall score regarding results of treatment. Tolerability was assessed on the basis of occurrences of adverse reaction throughout the study.

The results indicated that the degrees of joint pains and stiffness after treatment in Group A and Group B were lower than in Group C. The reduction of joint pains after treatment in Group A and Group B was significantly greater than that in Group C. The improvement of joint stiffness after treatment in Group A was slightly greater but not statistically significant against Group C. The improvement of joint pains and stiffness in Group B was significantly greater as compared to that in Group A and C. Thus, the study concluded that Rheumaneer had significant clinical efficacy in the treatment of joint pains and stiffness. This test was concluded October 1995.

It was an enormous achievement. The management of Nyonya Meneer, Charles in particular, felt relieved because their efforts and sacrifices had been paid off. Now Rheumaneer could be prescribed by doctors and used in hospitals. The next step was to make Rheumaneer widely available in the market.

The success of Rheumaneer passing clinical tests sparked new enthusiasm in the jamu industry and Indonesia in general. Soon after, the government was offering support through the Ministry of Health for clinical tests of jamu so that the national treasure could gain acceptance by medical professionals worldwide.

Furthermore, Dr. Sujudi, Minister of Health at the time, showed serious interest in advancing the jamu industry. He simplified standards for clinical tests to allow large numbers of companies to apply for testing.

One may argue that the future of the jamu industry is to transform itself into a phytomedicine industry. By being certified products, jamu would be equal competitors of modern pharmaceuticals, widening treatment options for patients, and benefitting medicine and health-care industry in general.

After a journey lasting almost nine years, Nyonya Meneer finally managed to launch Rheumaneer in the year 2000, as one of the phytomedicine products that had passed clinical and toxicity tests. The product was quickly granted a license from the Ministry of Health as a medication for curing rheumatism.

Rheumaneer could now be equated with modern medicine. Consumers' rights groups who were very concerned no longer needed to worry about consuming Rheumaneer as there existed a guarantee from the government outlining the advantages and the safety points of the product.

In April 2001, Rheumaneer was endorsed and officially approved by the Ministry of Health as suitable for consumers. It received its government registration number as a medicine that was safe to be taken internally. Nyonya Meneer's management and staff could not hide their happiness. Especially Charles. His dream to bolster the image of jamu had been realized.

On April 24, 2001, Nyonya Meneer signed a Memorandum of Understanding with a number of general hospitals and health clinics that had officially agreed to use and prescribe Rheumaneer. Implementation of the agreement began in May 2001, the company sent Rheumaneer to 180 hospitals and health clinics. Cooperation on the ground was so good that it could be said Rheumaneer became *the* medicine of choice for curing rheumatism, pains and inflammation of the joints, stiff and sore muscles, as well as fatigue and insomnia – all without chemicals and without side effects.

It must be noted that even though Rheumaneer was launched during the times of economic crisis, the product still performed extremely well. One of the factors was because the price was far below that of Western medicine – another factor was Rheumaneer had no contra-indications. It was not that surprising then that Nyonya Meneer revenue increased by 40% amidst the crisis. Furthermore, it was predicted revenue would increase regularly in the coming years.

To follow its success, Nyonya Meneer carried out research on another product, this time a jamu to prevent diabetes by reducing the level of glucose in the body. The company allocated billions of rupiah to fund this new project. The research is being performed by the Pharmaceutical and Medical Technology Application Center (P2TFM Center). The company is expecting another success story.

Nyonya Meneer had also approached the Council for Technology Exploration and Application (*Badan Pengkajian dan Penerapan*

Teknologi – BPPT) to work together developing the ingredients for the jamu. The company aimed to improve the quality of jamu by combining sophisticated technology but at the same time retaining its traditional characters. For this project, Nyonya Meneer allocated Rp 7.5 billion per annum.

Charles hoped this kind of cooperation would enable the benefits of jamu to be increasingly explored and give jamu a more significant role in society. He wanted many more jamu products to be clinically tested – and he will continue to work hard to align jamu with modern medicine.

Charles's promotion to President Director marked the first time the company was run by an educated professional. He realized that he now needed to follow the mantra of his Western counterparts: "The Customer is King." Charles established a customer service division, whose mandate is to ensure complete satisfaction for every customer. It started with trained employees who not only knew the products intimately, but who had a skill of communicating with all levels of society. All of the customer-facing staff was sent to a human resource development institute to speed up both their personal and professional growth.

Charles also revisited his relationships with his distributors to boost their efficiency and product knowledge even further, and by the middle of 1990s he made some modifications to their relationships with the company. His previous investments from years back resulted in dozens of loyal and dedicated partners and they were ready to work for him to expand their businesses even more. He brought in his biggest and most loyal agents and gave them direct access to his marketing team, as well as organized compulsory meetings to ensure the communication lines were static-free. By 1995, the company had 40 distributors covering 19 provinces, which sold through to 30,000 outlets.

Charles continued to favor international development and led the campaign to the Middle East. He studied the Saudi Arabian market in particular and discerned their preferences in tastes before custom-tailoring his jamu for export. Currently the company sells to over a dozen counties like the Philippines, Korea, the Netherlands, Taiwan, Japan, New Zealand, Sweden, and the United States.

The next trend seized by Nyonya Meneer in the early 1990s was multilevel marketing like Amway or Avon. Charles partnered with a Taiwanese company, Heaven Only International Co. Ltd. (HOI) and it has grown to become one of Nyonya Meneer's most successful international ventures to date. Interestingly, the reason given for the phenomenal success of Indonesian traditional medicine that is in direct competition with Chinese traditional medicine was explained by one of the Taiwanese partners as this: "Chinese medicine only cures, but Indonesian medicine prevents."

The next management crisis involved a dispute between Nonie's family and Charles. During the shareholders meeting in 1991, Nonie had resigned from the Board of Commissioners and her place was filled by her husband, Oke, until 1995. Nonie and Oke had six children but only three, Peter, Paul, and Tony had any involvement in the company. From Charles's side, his mother, Vera, and his sisters, Gwyneth and Fiona, were Commissioners. Each side owned 50% of the company.

In the beginning, both sides worked together to manage and build the company – perhaps strengthened by their loyalty to each other in the previous two conflicts. The problems started when Charles and his mother granted some shares to some parties outside the family. While not against the company's articles of association, Nonie's son, Tony, objected to the transfer and he stormed out of the shareholder meeting on August 12, 1995. The meeting had to be continued, though, as the quorum representatives of 133 shares out of 200 were present. As some of the shares were put as collateral with banks, the bankers had a right to vote as well. A resolution nominating Charles and Gwyneth as directors and Vera, Oke, and Fiona as commissioners was voted on and was passed. Even though the result was legal, Paul Saerang objected on the grounds that while the number of shares was equal, the representation on the Board of Directors and Commissioners were very skewed in Charles's favor.

As in the past, mediation was not successful and Tony, Nonie's son, filed a civil lawsuit against Charles in November 1995 in Semarang. Tony's claim was that Charles granted shares to an external party and he felt that only members of the family should hold them. Additionally, he wanted Charles to resign as President Director. After witnesses were called from both sides, the judge dismissed the case. Like his Uncle Hans, Tony appealed to the High Court as well as the Supreme Court but each time the appeal was dismissed.

After Tony's case was rejected, Nonie filed a suit in the District Court of Central Jakarta with the same case. After reviewing the case, on June 18, 1997 the judges bizarrely reversed the previous court's decision. In a preliminary decision, the court declared the previous board appointments not in line with the shareholders' agreement. The judges also pronounced Paul Saerang, Tony's brother, to replace Charles as President Director.

Charles was stunned. He couldn't believe that the position he held since 1989 was now in the hands of his cousin with little experience in running a business. In celebration of his newfound promotion, three days later, on June 21, 1997 Paul placed advertisements in major newspapers announcing Charles was no longer President Director of PT Nyonya Meneer and reminded all business partners not to engage in any transactions with him. Paul also mentioned in the advertisement that Lindawaty Suryadinata, Charles's wife, was appointed to the Board of Commissioners – causing speculations that there were marriage troubles between Lindawaty and Charles.

What shocked Charles even more was the fact that the case was still on appeal in the High Court and was far from final. He felt that his reputation was tarnished and was slandered in public, and he reported the advertisement to the District Police of Central Java. Charles's lawyer, Alexius Tantra Jaya, claimed that what Paul did was criminal and was causing unrest in a place of business. Furthermore, by announcing that Charles's wife was appointed to the Board of

Commissioners (without her knowledge or approval), Paul himself violated the company's articles of association as a change in directors can only be approved in a shareholders' meeting.

Nonie's family held the view that Charles and his father had been President Director for too long and it was time for her children to have a chance running it. Charles maintained the view that he didn't mind a change, as long as it followed proper procedures. As the conflict grew deeper and deeper, Charles decided the only way to settle this once and for all would be for one side to buy the other out. Anything short of that would surely lead the company to collapse.

Charles broached this matter with Nonie. She immediately rejected the idea of her selling out as Nyonya Meneer was the most important thing in her life since she was young. If anyone was to sell, it had to be Charles.

On July 3, 1997 Paul Saerang was summoned to the District Police Headquarters of Central Java to provide testimony. Paul admitted that he had made a mistake by making the announcement, and he was found guilty and spent one week in prison from November 24 to December 1, 1997. Newspapers around the country published stories of Paul's imprisonment and the experience changed him forever. Soon after his release, Nonie announced that this situation was out of control and she agreed to sell her shares to Charles. The only thing that now needed to be negotiated was the price. Both sides agreed they would appoint a neutral mediator to make this process less painful.

Another reason for this conflict stems from the fact that Nonie's family had been distributing Nyonya Meneer since the 1930s. Nonie's husband, Oke, was responsible for managing the business and after he passed away the business was passed to their third son, Peter.

As distributor and 50% shareholder, they demanded priority for delivery of product. However, it was the policy under Charles's leadership that priority went to distributors who ordered first, and further priority was given to those who paid on time. The Jakarta office was notorious for rejecting orders and payments were habitually late. Charles made the decision to stop supply until outstanding debts were settled.

John Himawan, the fifth child of Lucie Saerang, tried to be the mediator. John was never involved in the business, but as Nyonya Meneer's grandchild he felt he had an obligation to ensure the company would survive.

John began speaking with Tony, Nonie's fourth child but was met with a cold reception. Tony was not ready to make peace and did not agree to sell shares to Charles. John then contacted Charles, who readily accepted his role as mediator. Charles told him, "If you want to be the person, we will all say thank you."

John found the perfect opportunity to mediate at the wedding of Peter's son. The entire family was there, and John approached Tony once more. This time, Tony seemed to have a change of heart and was open to further discussions. John then met with Nonie who admitted that the court cases have caused her great grief, not to mention cost her substantial amounts of money. She agreed to meet with John and Charles to discuss the sale.

In June 1999, Nonie met Charles and John, and was accompanied by her grandson Raymond. Nonie told Charles, "I have spent millions of money in court, but the fact remains I always lost." She admitted that in her old age she wanted everything to be calm, especially with the death of her husband, Oke. Six months after the meeting, she passed away.

The negotiation process took about a year and a half. As both sides did not want to sit together, John dealt with each individually. Finally, on Charles's 15th wedding anniversary, a price had been reached. The share transfer would take place on October 27, 2000 in an executive club on Jl. Jenderal Sudirman. Payment was to be made in a bank on the ground floor. Only four people would be present: Peter Saerang, Charles, Vera Saerang, and John Himawan.

The share release went off without a hitch. For the first time since the death of the founder, all shares were held by one family. There were three shareholders: Charles, Vera and Gwyneth Roberts. Charles was finally firmly in control.

PEMBERITAHUAN

PT. PERINDUSTRIAN NYONYA MENEER, berkedudukan di Jl. Raden Patah No. 191-195, Semarang, yang dalam hal ini diwakili oleh Direksi yang baru sesuai Putusan Sela Pengadilan Negeri Jakarta Pusat No. 137/Pdt.G/1997/PN. Jkt.Pst. tanggal 18 Juni 1997, dengan ini memberitahukan kepada khalayak ramai bahwa dalam perkara Perdata No. 137/Pdt.G/1997/PN. JKT.Pst, pada Pengadilan Negeri Jakarta Pusat antara :

PT NYONYA MENEER sebagai Penggugat
melawan
DR. Charles Saerang (Ong Chen Chung) cs sebagai para Tergugat.

telah dijatuhkan Putusan Sela No. 137/Pdt.G/1997/PN. Jkt.Pst. tanggal 18 Juni 1997, yang amarnya berbunyi sebagai berikut :

MENGADILI

1. Mengabulkan gugatan Provisi Penggugat;
2. Memberhentikan Tergugat I, Tergugat II sebagai Direktur - Direktur dan Tergugat III, Tergugat IV dan Tergugat V sebagai Komisaris - Komisaris PT NYONYA MENEER yang tercatat dan tertuang dalam Berita Acara (Risalah) RUPS 1995 dan dikukuhkan dalam Berita Acara (Risalah) RUPS 1996 sebagaimana tercatat dalam Akte Berita Acara No. 66 tanggal 12 Agustus 1995 dan Akte Berita Acara No. 91 tanggal 9 Agustus 1996 yang dibuat oleh Notaris NY. JULIANA KARTINI SOEDJENDRO, SH.
3. Mengangkat Direksi dan Komisaris sementara PT NYONYA MENEER dengan susunan sebagai berikut :

   DIREKTUR   : PAUL SAERANG;
   KOMISARIS I   : PETER SAERANG;
   KOMISARIS II : NY. LINDAWATY SURYADINATA;

4. Menghukum Tergugat I s/d Tergugat V masing-masing membayar uang paksa sebesar Rp. 1.000.000,- (satu juta rupiah) per hari kepada Perseroan PT NYONYA MENEER apabila tidak mentaati Putusan Provisi ini;
5. Menangguhkan perihal biaya perkara hingga putusan akhir;

Sehubungan dengan Putusan Sela tersebut diperingatkan kepada khalayak ramai khususnya relasi bisnis untuk tidak mengadakan transaksi bisnis dan keuangan (business transactions and financial dealings) dengan Direksi yang sudah diberhentikan tersebut untuk menghindari terjadinya kesulitan-kesulitan hukum dikemudian hari; dan untuk selanjutnya semua hubungan bisnis dan transaksi keuangan PT Nyonya Meneer hanya dilakukan dengan Direksi baru sesuai Putusan Sela tersebut.

Demikian agar maklum adanya.

Jakarta, 19 Juni 1997
PT PERINDUSTRIAN NYONYA MENEER
ttd.
Paul Saerang
Direktur

An announcement in national newspaper, Suara Pembaruan, placed by Paul Saerang informing a change in Nyonya Meneer's management according to preliminary decision no.137, which dismissed Charles Saerang but appointed his wife, Lindawaty Suryadinata (without her knowledge or consent). This sparked a long dispute between Paul and Charles (1997).

PEMBERITAHUAN

Kantor Advokat dan Pengacara Qani Djemat & Partners, beralamat di Gedung Qani Djemat Plaza Lantai 8, Jalan Imam Bonjol No. 76 - 78, Jakarta Pusat, selaku kuasa dari Ny. Lindawaty Suryadinata, dengan ini memberitahukan kepada khalayak ramai bahwa :

Sehubungan dengan adanya pemberitaan melalui Iklan di beberapa Media Massa tentang Pemberitahuan Penggantian Direksi dan Komisaris PT. PERINDUSTRIAN NYONYA MENEER, atas pengangkatan Ny. Lindawaty Suryadinata sebagai Komisaris II perlu kiranya kami tegaskan bahwa klien kami selama ini tidak tahu menahu apalagi dimintai persetujuannya untuk duduk sebagai Komisaris II dengan demikian pengangkatan yang tercantum dalam pemberitahuan tersebut adalah tidak benar.

Demikian Pemberitahuan ini dibuat untuk diketahui oleh semua pihak yang berkepentingan.

Jakarta, 26 Juni 1997
Kuasa Ny. Lindawaty Suryadinata
Kantor Advokat & Pengacara
QANI DJEMAT & PARTNERS

ttd.   ttd.
DJAMHIR HAMZAH, SH   **ELIZABETH L. HAPSARI, SH**

PEMBERITAHUAN

Kantor Advokat dan Pengacara Qani Djemat & Partners, beralamat di Gedung Qani Djemat Plaza Lantai 8, Jalan Imam Bonjol No. 76 - 78 Jakarta Pusat, selaku kuasa dari Direksi dan Komisaris PT. PERINDUSTRIAN NYONYA MENEER, berkedudukan di Semarang, dengan ini memberitahukan kepada khalayak ramai bahwa :

1. Sehubungan dengan adanya pemberitaan melalui iklan di beberapa Media Massa tentang Pemberitahuan Penggantian Direksi dan Komisaris PT. PERINDUSTRIAN NYONYA MENEER, perlu kiranya diberitahukan bahwa Putusan Sela dari Pengadilan Negeri Jakarta Pusat atas perkara No. 137 /Pdt.G/1997/PN.Jkt.Pst pada tanggal 18 Juni 1997 belum mempunyai kekuatan hukum yang tetap karena terhadap putusan tersebut masih ada upaya hukum banding maupun kasasi, dengan demikian apabila ada pihak yang menggunakan Putusan Sela dari Pengadilan Negeri Jakarta Pusat atas perkara No. 137 /Pdt.G/1997/PN.Jkt.Pst tersebut.

2. Putusan hukum maupun tindakan Direksi dan Komisaris PT. PERINDUSTRIAN NYONYA MENEER berdasarkan akte Berita Acara No. 66 tanggal 12 Agustus 1995 dan Akte Berita Acara No. 91 tanggal 9 Agustus 1996 yang dibuat oleh Notaris Ny. Juliana Kartini Soedjendro, SH adalah tetap sah.

Demikian Pemberitahuan ini dibuat untuk diketahui oleh semua pihak yang berkepentingan.

Jakarta, 26 Juni 1997
Kuasa Direksi dan Komisaris
PT. PERINDUSTRIAN NYONYA MENEER
Kantor Advokat & Pengacara
QANI DJEMAT & PARTNERS

ttd.   ttd.
DJAMHIR HAMZAH, SH   **ELIZABETH L. HAPSARI, SH**

Announcement by the lawyers of Lindawaty Suryadinata, declaring that she had not known or consented to her appointment as Commissioner II of Nyonya Meneer (June 26, 1997).

118

Saerang vs Saerang
Putusan Sela Berbuntut ke Kasus Pidana

Semarang, Bernas

Pemuatan iklan pemberitahuan putusan sela Pengadilan Negeri (PN) Jakarta Pusat bagi kasus perdata di PT Perindustrian Nyonya Meneer Semarang berbuntut ke kasus pidana.

Pasalnya, Dr Charles Saerang mengadukan Paul Saerang ke Direktorat Reserse Polda Jateng, karena telah menista (mencemarkan) melalui tulisan, serta melakukan perbuatan tidak menyenangkan yang berakibat timbulnya keresahan para karyawan.

Pengaduan Charles Saerang melalui kuasa hukumnya, Alexius Tantrajaya SH ke Polda Jateng dilakukan sehari setelah pemuatan pemberitahuan di media massa, 21 Juni lalu, kata Kadit Serse Polda Jateng, Kolonel Pol Drs Ansyaad Mbai kepada wartawan, Senin (30/6).

"Polda memang sudah menerima pengaduan Charles Saerang yang disampaikan kuasa hukumnya, dan saat ini kasusnya masih dalam proses pemeriksaan. Paul Saerang sudah datang ke Polda Jateng, Sabtu (28/6)," kata Kolonel Ansyaad.

Kasus pengaduan tersebut, kata Kadit Serse, sesuai pengaduannya, yaitu perbuatan menista melalui tulisan maupun perbuatan tidak menyenangkan dan berakibat timbulnya keresahan pada karyawan, adalah perbuatan pidana. Dari kasus tersebut termasuk pasal 310 KUHP (menista) dan pasal 335 KUHP (perbuatan yang tidak menyenangkan).

Menurut Tantrajaya SH, alasan pengaduan tersebut karena putusan sela kasus perdata oleh PN Jakarta Pusat itu sebenarnya belum mempunyai kekuatan hukum. Apalagi kemudian muncul perubahan susunan direksi baru, yang tidak sesuai anggaran dasar atau melalui RUPS (rapat umum pemegang saham).

"Jelas pemuatan pemberitahuan melalui media massa itu tidak sah, karena putusan tersebut tidak sesuai dengan AD/ART atau pun melalui RUPS. Bahkan secara jelas Paul Saerang telah mencemarkan nama baik klien saya, yaitu melalui tulisan tersebut. Bahkan adanya pengumuman tersebut juga berakibat timbulnya keresahan para karyawan," katanya.

Charles Saerang mengatakan, pada waktu pengambilan putusan 'pergantian' dan pengangkatan direksi, ternyata istrinya, Ny Lindawaty Suryadinata sedang di luar negeri. "Istri saya tidak tahu menahu, apalagi sampai diangkat menjadi komisaris II," kata Charles melalui kuasa hukumnya.

Ansyaad ditanya pengaduan Charles Saerang yang terkait dengan kasus perdata yang saat ini sedang dalam proses banding tersebut berdiri sendiri. Artinya tidak harus menunggu putusan banding.

"Kasus ini lepas dari kasus perdata yang disidangkan di Jakarta. Karena itu kita jalan terus untuk memprosesnya, dan Paul Saerang sebagai tersangka sudah kita periksa," kata Kadit Serse.

Dijelaskan, saat ini sedang dilakukan pemeriksaan terhadap Paul Saerang. Tapi tersangka belum perlu ditahan, meski sesuai dengan pasal 335 KUHP tersangka itu bisa dikenakan tahanan.

"Kami belum melakukan penahanan, karena sampai sekarang proses pemeriksaan masih berjalan lancar. Kecuali nanti mengalami kesulitan," jelas Kadit Serse. (rif)

"Preliminary decision resulted in criminal acts" (Bernas, 1997).

Pabrik Jamu Nyonya Meneer Diduga Menggelapkan Pajak

Jakarta, Bernas

DPR: Tindaklanjuti Temuan Itu!

Jakarta, Bernas

"Nyonya Meneer is suspected of embezzlement" and then
"People's Representative Council: 'Investigate Further the Findings!'" (Bernas, 1997).

Sebuah Perusahaan Jamu Diduga Sebarkan Komunisme

Amidst the disputes between Charles and Paul, the company's bulletin was suspected to spread the teachings of Karl Marx, simply by including the philosopher in an article on the people who changed world economy. This story is possibly paid for by an interested party. (Republika, 1997).

Geger Nyonya Meneer Kini Kembali Mencuat

Merasa Dicemarkan, Charles Mejahijaukan Paul

Paul Saerang taken to prison (Jawa Pos, 1997).

Nyonya Meneer rugi Rp 450 juta akibat sengketa pemilik saham

SEMARANG (Bisnis): PT Nyonya Meneer (NM) Semarang menderita kerugian Rp 450 juta akibat merosotnya kepercayaan pasar, menyusul sengketa antarpemilik saham perusahaan jamu terbesar di Jateng tersebut.

Direktur NM Charles Saerang mengatakan kerugian perusahaan disebkan oleh pengumuman putusan sela Pengadilan Negeri Jakarta atas sengketa saham NM oleh Paul Saerang melalui sejumlah media massa empat bulan lalu yang menimbulkan penilaian buruk masyarakat atas perusahaan.

"Akibat pengumuman putusan sela yang ditambahi kalimat oleh terdakwa [Paul Saerang] itu menimbulkan kerugian material dengan nilai Rp 450 juta maupun kerugian moral," ujarnya saat memberikan kesaksian pada kasus sengketa NM di Pengadilan Negeri Semarang, kemarin.

Sidang keempat tersebut menampilkan dua saksi korban yaitu Charles Saerang (Dirut PT NM) dan Harianto (sales manager PT NM) guna diminta keterangan atas dakwaam kepada Paul Saerang, direktur NM.

Menurut Charles, akibat pengumuman di mass media oleh Paul yang berisi a.l. pemberhentian Charles Saerang sebagai Dirut itu juga berisi permintaan kepada para relasi agar tidak mengadakan transaksi bisnis serta keuangan dengan direksi yang sudah diberhentikan.

Setelah pengumuman itu, lanjutnya, selama empat minggu kemudian terjadi penunggakan pembayaran dari sejumlah agen dan distributor yang tersebar di Jateng, Jabar, Jatim, Sumatra, Kalimantan, Jakarta dan Malaysia sehingga menimbulkan kerugian sebesar Rp 450 bagi NM.

Charles menjelaskan, saat ini dia secara resmi masih menjabat sebagai Dirut NM yang diangkat melalui kesepakatan rapat umum pemegang saham (RUPS) perusahaan jamu itu pada 28 Januari 1991.

"Kalau terdapat kesalahan saya siap diberhentikan, tapi tentunya sesuai ketentuan yang berlaku (RUPS)," tandasnya.

Sementara itu, saksi korban II Haryanto mengatakan dengan adanya kasus tersebut, sampai saat ini penjualan produk belum normal 100%. "Beberapa agen distributor masih menunggu perkembangan kasus itu terselesaikan."

Akibat pengumuman yang belum meliki kekuatan hukum itu, Charles bahkan, perusahaannya selain kerugian terial berupa kemerosotan omzet pada secara pribadi juga menderita kerugian moral berupa pencemaran nama baik.

"Saya sangat malu, terhina dan dicemarkan masyarakat umum serta rekan bisnis kan sempat pula mengguncang kehidupan nisan keluarga kami," tandasnya.

Dia mengemukakan untuk menghadapi dampak lebih lanjut pihaknya mengambil beberapa langkah, seperti meminkan dan mengadakan pendekatan ngan relasi, pegawai dan distributor hingga melibatkan Walikota Semarang.

"Namun upaya itu belum membuahkan hasil optimal, terbukti masih banyaknya gakan dari agen maupun distributor di Indonesia dan Malaysia." (k21)

"Nyonya Meneer suffers 450 million in losses due to shareholders' disputes"
(Bisnis Indonesia, 1997).

Majalah Potret

Jamu, Marx, dan Kejati

Pimpinan PT Nyonya Meneer dipanggil kejaksaan gara-gara artikel tentang Karl Marx. Padahal, artikel itu dikutip dari buku terbitan Gramedia.

PERUSAHAAN jamu Nyonya Meneer tampaknya sedang mengidap "pegal linu". Selain menghadapi cekcok keluarga yang dampaknya merongrong manajemen (lihat rubrik *Ekonomi & Bisnis* halaman 95) masih ada majalah *Potret*, yang menyebabkan direksinya berurusan dengan Kejaksaan Tinggi Jawa Tengah. Hal itu terjadi Senin pekan lalu di Semarang.

Pangkal persoalan terletak pada *Potret* terbitan Juni 1989. Berkala yang tak diperjualbelikan itu memuat teori Karl Marx. Judulnya: *Karl Marx*, sepanjang enam halaman, mengungkapkan pikiran-pikiran Marx, termasuk biografi singkatnya.

Di situ disebutkan bagaimana Marx mengkritik ekonomi kapitalis yang mengilhami Lenin, Mao, dan Castro untuk mencetuskan revolusi. Disebutkan juga *Manifesto Partai Komunis* dan kutipan tulisan Alexander Solzhenitsyn dari buku *Gulag Archipelago*, yang menceritakan Soviet di bawah Stalin.

Gara-gara artikel Karl Marx itu, Charles Ong, Pemimpin Umum merangkap Penanggung Jawab dan Pemimpin Redaksi *Potret* periode 1987–1990, diminta keterangan. Juga Hambar Sinoeng, pengganti

Charles Ong. "Kabarnya, fotokopi majalah edisi Juni kini beredar luas," kata Arno Gutama Harjono, pengacara Charles, yang di PT Nyonya Meneer menduduki jabatan direktur.

"Padahal, kami sudah menarik edisi itu saat sedang beredar," ujar Arno. Bahkan, setelah majalah itu ditarik, pihak Nyonya Meneer melapor pada Badan Koordinasi Bantuan Pemantapan Stabilitas Nasional Daerah, pengacara muda dari Jakarta itu, seluk-beluk artikel itu. "Pemeriksaan dihentikan karena klien kami tidak terbukti menyebarluaskan ajaran Marxisme," kata Arno, pengacara muda dari Jakarta itu.

Keterangan Arno bukan tidak berdasar. Artikel Karl Marx yang dipersoalkan Kejati itu, ternyata, berupa nukilan dari buku *Tokoh-Tokoh Ekonomi Mengubah Dunia* terbitan Gramedia. Dan sejak terbit tahun 1988 silam, buku itu belum pernah dilarang. "Sampai saat ini, Gramedia belum mendapat larangan atau teguran dari mana pun," kata Sudiran, bagian pemasaran PT Gramedia. Buku karya Paul Heinz Koesters yang dialihbahasakan oleh Titi Soentoro Efendi itu sudah laku 1.300 eksemplar.

Sebenarnya, tulisan mengenai pikiran-pikiran Karl Marx adalah sambungan dari dua edisi sebelumnya. Berturut-turut *Potret* menyadur bab-bab lain dari buku yang sama. Bab I, misalnya, membahas pikiran-pikiran pakar ekonomi Adam Smith dan bab II mengulas teori-teori David Ricardo. "Kami sudah meminta izin pada Gramedia untuk menyadurnya," kata Arno.

Dirjen PPG Subrata ternyata belum mendengar kasus *Potret* tersebut. "Tapi tidak masalah kalau kejaksaan yang menemukan artikel itu. Toh masih kejaksaan yang melaporkan k Deppen," ujar Subrata. Karena laporan itu belum ada, Subrata belum mengira tindakan yang mungkin diambil telah pencabutan STT. "Juga apa diteliti latar belakang penulisan artikel itu," katanya.

"Kalau ini, tampaknya, tidak akan terjongkang oleh hukum pidana. Menurut pasal 78 KUHP, tuntutan hukum bagi pelanggaran atau kejahatan yang dilakukan dengan memperginakan percetakan gugur setelah lewat dari satu tahun. Artikel itu terbit dua tahun yang lalu. Sedangkan *Potret* terbit sebulan sekali, untuk kepentingan intern

perusahaan, tebalnya sekitar 100 halaman warna, edisi luks dan hanya dicetak 400 eksemplar untuk tiap nomor.

Bunga V., Nasik Isnaini, dan Haddy Lugito (Semarang)

"Jamu, Marx, and the Chief Prosecutor's Office: The director of Nyonya Meneer was summoned to the Chief Prosecutor's office due to an article on Karl Marx; even though the article was only quoting a book published by Gramedia" (Tempo, 1997).

Charles motivating the factory workers (circa 1999).

*Charles and Sri Redjeki, former Minister for the Empowerment of Women,
visited the factory at Jalan Kaligawe, Semarang (circa 2000).*

122

BUKAN PENGUNGSI. Ini bukan pengungsi Aceh atau pun Ambon, tetapi para pengunjuk rasa dari PT Nyonya Meneer Semarang. Sekitar 1500 orang buruh perusahaan itu melakukan aksi dan nginep di gedung DPRD I Jateng. Berita selengkapnya di halaman 4. (Foto : Wawasan/Mic Soekanto)

• Pagi tadi urunan uang untuk beli nasi bungkus

Karyawan Nyonya Meneer 'nginap' di DPRD

"Nyonya Meneer's Workers Spend the Night at the Regional People's Representative Council (Dewan Perwakilan Rakyat Daerah – DPRD)" (2000).

Nyonya Meneer employees on a solidarity rally (February 7, 2000).

An official from the Organization for the Deliberations of the District Leaders
(Musyawarah Pimpinan Kecamatan – *Muspika) addressed the laborers of Nyonya Meneer*
after their rally (February 10, 2000).

Charles joining the workers for a free lunch, celebrating his 51st birthday (2003).

124

The newspaper clippings and their readable headlines:

PRODUCT SHOWCASE

"Jamu" May Improve After Birth Looks

RAGAM

BPPT-Nyonya Meneer Sepakat Kembangkan Kultur Jaringan

An article in an English-language newspaper on Nyonya Meneer's post-partum medicinal products, a sign of success of the company's export (2001).

Nyonya Meneer and the Council for the Study and Application of Technology agree to develop tissue culture (Suara Pembaruan, 2000).

Nyonya Meneer sponsored "Kereta Kids" (kids' train) — an event where children could ride a small train with celebrities — as an attempt to break into the children's market (2000).

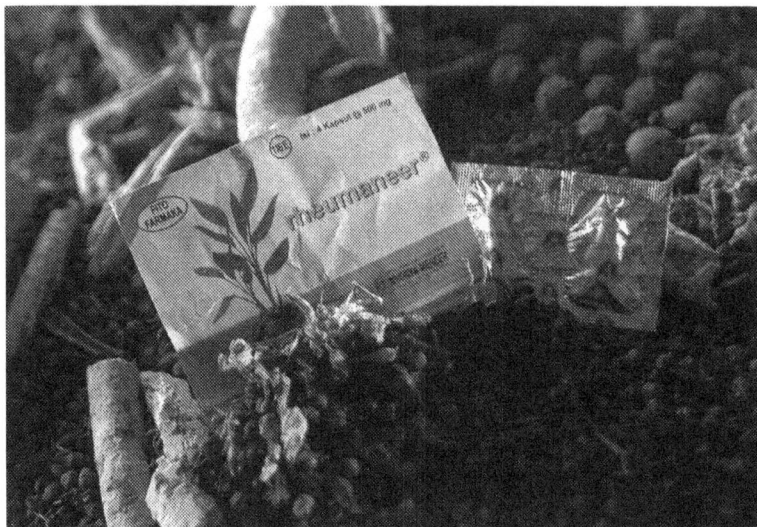

Rheumaneer, a product for curing rheumatism, one of the phytomedicine products that passed clinical and toxicity tests (see Case Study in Chapter IV).

An advertisement for Rheumaneer featuring Ikang Fawzi, a famous musician and actor (2001).

Fitofarmaka digunakan untuk kedokteran

SEMARANG (Bisnis): PT Nyonya Meneer (NM) meloloskan satu jenis produk fitofarmaka untuk digunakan dalam dunia kedokteran, sementara industri jamu tersebut mematok target penjualan pada 2000 sebesar Rp 7,8 miliar atau naik 25,8% dari realisasi 1999 Rp 6,2 miliar.

Menurut Neni Kardiana, juru bicara NM, mengatakan produk fitofarmaka dari perusahaannya telah mendapatkan rekomendasi lolos uji klinis dan uji toksin dari Depkes untuk digunakan di dunia kedokteran mulai tahun 2000.

"Produk yang mendapat rekomendasi Depkes itu adalah *rheumaneer*, yaitu jenis fitofarmaka untuk penyembuhan penyakit rheumatik," ujarnya di sela-sela acara Tarwih Keliling di Graha Sari, belum lama ini.

Dia menjelaskan inovasi produk itu mampu meningkatkan nilai penjualan perusahaan yang ditargetkan pada 1999 sebesar Rp 6,2 miliar itu sudah tercapai pada bulan November. "Untuk itu kami pada tahun 2000 menaikkan target sekitar 25,8% menjadi Rp 7,2 miliar," tuturnya. **(bar)**

An article announcing that Rheumaneer has passed as a phytomedicine that may be prescribed by doctors (Bisnis Indonesia, 1999).

Rheumaneer: the first jamu in Indonesia to pass clinical tests. The article explains the symptoms of rheumatism and how Rheumaneer can treat them (2000).

An advertisement promoting Rheumaneer to senior citizens who often suffer from muscle and joint pains (2000).

*The new head office of Nyonya Meneer, Gedung Multiguna 2020,
at Jl. Raden Patah no.191-199, Semarang.
The building was opened February 20, 2004, coinciding with Charles Saerang's 52th birthday.
It stands next to the old factory and Rumah Abu, the house where Nyonya Meneer used to live.*

Inside the new factory (2004).

Meneer Café in Ciputra Mall (2004).

Meneer Café in Senayan Trade Center (2004).

A limited edition of stamps dedicated to Nyonya Meneer, released in 2004.

*Charles and the management of Heaven Only International (HOI)
at the signing of the Memorandum of Understanding of Multilevel Marketing
of jamu products in Taichung, Taiwan (2007).*

The Garden of Medicinal Herbs at Jalan Raya Semarang, Bawen.

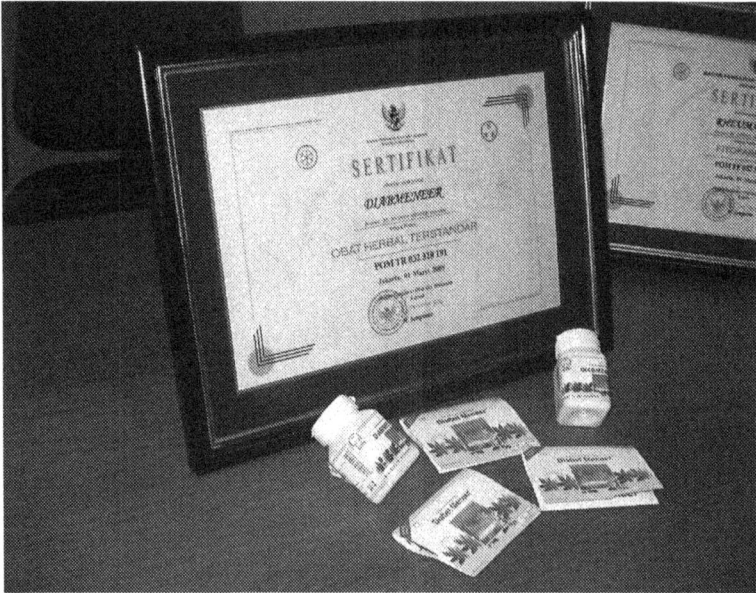

*Certificate for Diabmeneer, a product to treat diabetes,
for passing the standardized herbal medicine criteria (2005).*

*A recent ad campaign for Amurat, a new product that controls uric acid, featuring Tukul Arwana,
a fast rising comedian (2007).*

At the Opening Ceremony of the Fifth National Deliberation of the Association of Jamu and Traditional Medicine Entrepreneurs (Munas V GP Jamu) with President Susilo Bambang Yudhoyono (April 12, 2007).

Also at the Opening Ceremony of Munas V GP Jamu. From left to right: Charles (also Chairman of GP Jamu), Siti Fadilah Supari (Minister of Health), President Yudhoyono.

From left to right: Siti Fadilah Supari, MS Hidayat (Chief of the Indonesian Chamber of Commerce), First Lady Ani Yudhoyono, President Yudhoyono, and Charles. In his opening speech the President said, "Someday I would like to be a salesperson for jamu and Indonesian traditional medicine."

CHAPTER FIVE
THE FUTURE OF NYONYA MENEER

THERE IS a Chinese saying about family businesses: the father builds it, the son expands it, and the grandson destroys it. That saying was constantly in Charles's head during each of the crises and he swore to himself it would not happen to his grandmother's company.

For the future, Charles commits himself to further grow the company and have it bring even greater pride to the management, workers, and the larger society. In 2004, the company inaugurated a new head office, Gedung Multiguna 2020, at Jl. Raden Patah no.191-199, Semarang, next to Nyonya Meneer's old house. This charming building is equipped with testing labs, health and psychiatric clinics, a library, and Meneer Café. Now that facilities are already upgraded, the management looks to improve their human resources. To achieve this goal, the company will provide more training for accomplished employees as well as hold other professional development programs. Charles wants to ensure that the workers feel even prouder and happier to be part of the big family of Nyonya Meneer.

Charles has also set up a specialized Public Relations division to further spread the company's good name and bring the company closer to the people. This division will devote itself to strategic communications, including developing core values, corporate culture, and corporate mindset. On top of that, the company will implement a new distribution and marketing plan: the National Product Strategy, which entails looking at each of their distributors, recognizing the ten with the best track record, and then assigning one product to each of them as their concentration. For example, one distributor will only be selling the Awet Ayu line in all its forms (powder, pill, cream, capsule, etc.). It is expected that, with a much narrower focus, the distributor's efficiency as well as sales of each product will increase. If all goes well, Charles even envisages taking the company public, a significant move that he hopes will improve the control of the company as well as refine its image.

However, growing the company must go hand-in-hand with increasing awareness and desirability of its products. As mentioned in the Rheumaneer case study, Charles's ambition as a jamu entrepreneur is to boost the popularity of jamu worldwide and have it earn the same level of respect as conventional medicine. Therefore, Charles will keep cooperating with competent scientific institutions to research, test, and create new jamu products. There is much about the efficacy of jamu and its ingredients that needs to be brought into the larger public's awareness. For example, the herb *daun sambiloto* (green chireta) has been proven to slow the spread of intestinal tumors. Research and discoveries such as this have been made – by companies as well as other institutions – but there is still a lack of governmental and commercial effort in bringing these findings to light.

The next step will be to get the Ministry of Research and Technology to officially endorse such findings. Once there is reliable scientific evidence on the efficacy of jamu, upheld by respected specialists, even

those skeptical toward using traditional medicine may start to take interest in jamu – and feasibly, in time they will grow confidence in its healing powers and become regular users. Certainly this will bring in new
customers to the jamu industry as well as add fame to Indonesia, the
country of origin of hundreds of varieties of the ingredients.

In order to achieve that aim, Charles will keep lobbying academics, medical professionals, and the government consistently to get them
more seriously interested in developing jamu. He has endeavored to re-
position the jamu industry from under the Food and Drugs Supervisory
Council (*Badan Pengawas Obat dan Makanan* – BPOM) to under the
General Directory, or to become a special division under the Ministry
of Health with the final goal of having research facilities, doctors, and
hospitals specializing in jamu. Additionally, Charles will proceed to have
discussions with health insurance companies about providing coverage
for purchasing jamu. By garnering the support of modern professionals
and institutions, Charles is confident that this precious traditional treasure will be able to sail successfully into the era of globalization.

Indeed, Charles has his eyes firm on expanding the presence of
jamu in the international market. He is convinced that foreign demand
and sales will only get larger, especially because of the natural and green
living trend that is very much in fashion in many parts of the world
today. People from all over the globe are getting more and more curious
about herbs and natural medication.

Seizing the opportunity, Charles arranges to open a Jamu Garden in
2008, situated in Jl. Soekarno-Hatta km.3, Karang Jati. This garden will
build on the accomplishments of the 2.3 hectare Garden of Medicinal
Herbs established in 1981. The first garden grew more than 250 species
of medicinal herbs, cultivated for jamu's raw materials, for preservation
of the plants themselves, for research, and other purposes. In time, the
garden burgeoned to become a pride of the community. Many earned

their degrees by researching the plants in the garden. It also created job opportunities as Nyonya Meneer hired farmers to work on the garden as well as held experiments in biotechnology.

The new Jamu Garden will allow the company to do what could not be done in the original garden. For example, the new garden will be open for agro-tourism. It will cultivate rare and endangered medicinal plant species from all over Indonesia; each of the 32 provinces will donate a plant particular to their region. Thus, visitors can see all the different varieties of plants without having to travel from Sabang to Merauke. Just as the original garden, the new Jamu Garden will also serve educational purposes. There will be a laboratory dedicated to research on medicinal plants, which will be opened to the public. There will also be a theater to house a myriad of presentations and educational programs. A miniature of Nyonya Meneer's production process will also be displayed so that visitors can learn about the workings of the factory without having to visit it. Even more excitingly, the company is preparing to specially cultivate Nyonya Meneer-branded raw materials – such as ginseng or *temulawak* (round turmeric rhizomes), grown in this garden and cared by experts – and then sell them to international markets.

By all means, the company's foreign market shares are increasing. Until recently, Nyonya Meneer has reaped success in the following countries: China, United States, Brunei Darussalam, Malaysia, Vietnam, Philippines, Japan, Korea, Singapore, Taiwan, New Zealand, and Saudi Arabia. However, since the company did much research, development, and product diversification, they have succeeded to market their products to these countries as well: Nigeria, Namibia, Republic of Benin, North Africa, Togo, Cameroon, Ivory Coast, Argentina, and Brazil.

The vision doesn't end there. Nyonya Meneer is also embracing the digital era. The company has joined some of the world's major business portals, giving access to potential customers to learn about

Nyonya Meneer. Online orders from all over the world are also accepted. The company has collaborated with international couriers, such as FedEx and DHL, as well as established online merchants, such as Amazon.com, to make it easier for customers abroad to purchase Nyonya Meneer's products.

There are also intentions to enhance their multilevel marketing in Taiwan. Demand for Nyonya Meneer's products in Taiwan alone exceeds one million dollars per month. This figure will only increase, as there are new demands for natural cosmetics and traditional herbal drinks in addition to the regular demands of curative and preventative jamu.

Nyonya Meneer will also strengthen their relationships with their strategic business partners. For example, they are working together with a hospital in California that uses and prescribes their products to patients. The hospital has branches all over the United States, which signals that demand will soar to new heights. The hospital also has an online ordering system, allowing people everywhere to purchase Nyonya Meneer's products from the convenience of their home.

Passing the very demanding health standards of the United States is a testament to the quality of Nyonya Meneer's products. This certainly adds value to the products and allows them to compete with the currently more well-known Chinese products. Demand from the United States exceeds two million dollars per month.

Yet there are more exciting developments on the horizon. The company intends to invite and work with Indonesian embassies and trade attachés abroad to help introduce jamu in their host countries. Nyonya Meneer will also build relationships with foreign embassies in Indonesia and get them interested to try jamu products and introduce them in their home countries. Research and analysis are also being performed on consumer characteristics in many countries to better understand the preferences and behaviors of consumers in different countries.

With commitment and dedication to these strategies, Nyonya Meneer is confident to be the international trendsetter of traditional medicine, 100% free of chemicals.

Through its triumphs and tragedies, Nyonya Meneer has managed to defy its critics and build one of the strongest jamu brands in the country. As the third generation in command, Charles proved himself to be a visionary who cares deeply about the company, the jamu industry, and the country's economy. He dreams of an "Indonesia Incorporated," a synergy where academics, professionals, businesspeople, the government and all parties work jointly to realize a conducive and profitable environment, not only for industries, but also for the country's prosperity. His knowledge and skills he applies not only within his own company, but he also shares them by teaching (he taught at Diponegoro University and 17 Agustus University in Semarang and at the University of Hawaii in the United States), delivering talks, and writing articles (he had a special column called "The Business Management of Charles Saerang" from 1993-1995 in *Kedaulatan Rakyat*). He also joined the Association of Jamu and Traditional Medicine Entrepreneurs (*Gabungan Pengusaha Jamu dan Obat Tradisional* – GP Jamu), an organization that looked after the interests of all the jamu entrepreneurs in Indonesia. Active since the organization's founding, he was appointed Chairman in 1999. For his lifelong dedication to the jamu industry in particular and marketing theory in general, Charles has received many awards and distinctions.

In Nyonya Meneer, he built on his grandmother's legacy as the first woman entrepreneur in Indonesia and transformed her company to become the largest traditional jamu enterprise in the country. Even though the odds were decidedly against a successful management transition, Nyonya Meneer has disproved the Chinese saying about family business and will no doubt continue to thrive for many generations to come.

PRODUCT LIST

NEW PRODUCTS

No. 118 JAMU AMURAT

*Helps alleviate muscle pains and soreness of the joints.
(also available in capsules)*

No. 116 E RHEUMANEER

*A phytomedicine product that cures rheumatism, muscle
stiffness and soreness.*

No. 122 DIABMENEER

*These herbal extract capsules are specially formulated to
reduce sugar level in the blood.*

No. 128 D LANGSINGNEER

*Facilitates defecation without causing gastrointestinal
discomforts or diarrhea, helps improve health in general.*

No. 124 D TEMUMENEER

*Helps maintain healthy liver function and digestion, relieves
rheumatic symptoms.*

TEMULAWAK

*Maintains healthy liver function, improves digestion and
blood circulation, increases the body's vitality and immune
system, enhances general well-being.*

V-NEER

A delicately fragrant and gentle deodorizing mist specially formulated for everyday intimate feminine use. It contains Piperis folium *extract, a natural antiseptic.*

No. 126 MINYAK KAYU PUTIH

This product helps relieve stomach pains, itches from insect and mosquito bites, and nausea.

I. HERBS FOR WOMEN AND GIRLS

A. Health and Beauty Care

No. 26 JAMU PATMOSARI

(herbs for slimming and trimming the body)
Formulated for women to maintain a slim, firm, and healthy body. Helps regulate blood circulation, improving the skin tone. Especially effective when taken twice a week after menstruation.

No. 48 JAMU GADIS REMAJA

(herbs for young women)
Especially formulated for teenage girls who just started menstruating. Used regularly, these herbs provide the best beauty care for a young body. Keeps the body slim and the skin smooth and radiant. It is a health-aid for the young woman's rapidly developing body.
(also available in pills)

No. 50 JAMU GALIAN SARI

(herbs for women to maintain a slim body)
For women to keep a slim, firm body and a smooth, radiant facial skin. May be used as both a health- and beauty-aid.

No. 64 JAMU GALIAN PUTRI

(herbs for those entering womanhood)
For girls who want to preserve a slim and healthy body and a glowing face. To be taken three times a week after menstruation.
(also available in pills)

No. 85 JAMU GALIAN SINGSET

(herbs to rejuvenate skin)
Herbs that help slim and firm the female body and restore a more youthful appearance.
(also available in pills and capsules)

No. 103 JAMU SRIKATON

(herbs for after childbirth)
Gives special care for the mother's body after giving birth. Strengthens the uterus, helps prevent excessive vaginal discharge, regulates blood circulation, slims the stomach and waistline, and makes the face radiant.
(also available in pills)

No. 106 A JAMU AWET MUDA A

(herbs for ever-youthful appearance)
A rejuvenating herbal mixture for women. Refreshes and beautifies the skin. To be taken regularly in the morning.
(also available in capsules)

No. 106 B JAMU AWET MUDA B

(herbs for ever-youthful appearance)
A complementary formula to Awet Muda A that helps make the face and body look and feel forever young. To be taken regularly in the afternoon.
(also available in capsules)

B. For Healing Feminine Ailments
No. 4 JAMU DILEP I

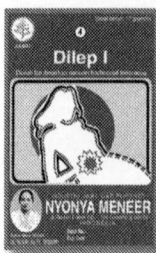

(herbs for menstrual pains)
Assists with abdominal cramps and facial pallor due to poor blood flow during menstruation. These special herbs increase the flow of blood and continue to regulate it.

No. 5 JAMU DILEP II

(herbs for menstrual pains)
To be used by women during menstruation who experience headaches, backaches, and cramps due to excessive blood flow. Effective in decreasing the loss of blood.

No. 17 JAMU PEPUTIH

(herbs for yeast infection)
Herbal remedy for vaginal discharge. For chronic condition, this jamu should be taken daily, whereas temporary sufferers should take it three times a week.
(also available in pills and capsules)

No. 30 JAMU DATANG BULAN TIDAK COCOK

(herbs to regulate menstrual cycle)
Herbal remedy for women with an irregular menstrual cycle.
(also available in pills)

No. 27 JAMU PIL NIFAS AMPLOP

(herbs for menstrual disorders)
These herbs have been specially prepared for women who are missing their menstrual periods, although they are not pregnant. These herbs facilitates regular menstrual cycle and ensures a healthy womb.
Caution: Pregnant women should not take these herbs.

C. For the Bride
No. 51 JAMU GALIAN KEMANTEN

(herbs for the bride)
Special herbs for the newly-wed bride and those about to be married. Enhance health and fitness, firm the stomach and the body, impart youthful and radiant complexion.

D. Special Herbs for Women
No. 87 JAMU RAHIM SEHAT

(herbs to strengthen the uterus)
Herbs that strengthen the uterus. Should be taken by those prone to miscarriages.
(also available in pills)

No. 97 JAMU BIBIT

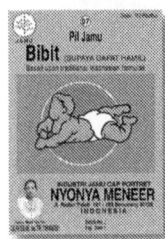

(herbs to promote fertility)
Should be taken regularly by women who experience difficulties in becoming pregnant. These herbs promote fertility, however, they should not be taken if menstruation occurs irregularly.
(also available in pills)

II. HERBS FOR BEAUTY

A. Jamu for Beauty Care
No. 9 JAMU SEHAT WANITA

(herbs for women's health maintenance)
Formulated for women who want to maintain their health and fitness. These herbs are especially good for the stomach; also provide for youthful vigor throughout a woman's life.
(also available in pills)

No. 18 JAMU AWET AYU

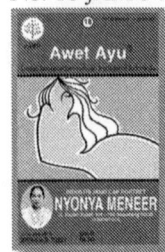

(herbs for healthy clear complexion)
A special combination of herbs to refresh the female body. Used regularly, it keeps the skin clean and healthy and beautifies the complexion. Also helps regulate menstruation and renews the body's energy. Awet Ayu herbs should be taken daily, especially following one's menstrual period.
(also available in pills and capsules)

No. 18 B LULUR AWET AYU

(herbs to apply to body for skin care)
A very fine powder used for ages by beautiful Javanese women to care for their skin. When used regularly, this traditional beauty-aid both softens and tightens facial and body skin, as well as prevents wrinkles. It also imparts a delicate fragrance while keeping the complexion looking young, clean, and attractive.

No. 18 C LULUR AWET AYU CREAM

(herbal cream for natural skin care)
Lulur Awet Ayu cream is a traditional beauty cream for facial and body care. It will make the skin tighter, smooth, healthier, shiny, fragrant, and fresh.

No. 49 JAMU GALIAN CEPAKA PUTIH

(herbs for women to renew energy)
A perfect combination of herbs prepared for women who are underweight, pale, weak, and susceptible to illness. Specially designed for those who feel they are no longer attractive and have lost their sex appeal. Helps replace lost energy and keeps the body looking radiant and healthy. Take daily until the body is rejuvenated.

No. 81 MANGIR HARUM

(herbal mask)
An herbal compound that is to be softened with water and used as a body mask. Softens, cleanses, and eliminates skin coarseness and blemishes.

No. 81 A MANGIR CREAM

(moisturizer from mangir)
Mangir Cream is used as a foundation and acts as a moisturizing cream. It is manufactured from flowers and other herbal ingredients which are good for facial skin and overall beauty care. Regular use will make the face look smooth, youthful, fresh, and clean.

No. 88 JAMU JERAWAT

(herbs to treat acne)
A special herbal concoction that works internally to rid the skin of acne. It keeps the skin smooth and healthy.

No. 94 JAMU MEKAR SARI

(herbs for breast toning)
These herbs should be taken to firm sagging breasts and give them a full, sexy shape.

No. 96 JAMU DEWI KECANTIKAN

(herbs for beauty-aid)
Herbs that enhance the beauty of the face and body. Prevents wrinkles, beautifies complexion, and imparts that glowing, youthful look desired by women. These herbs also slim and firm the body, especially the stomach.
(also available in pills)

B. Cosmetics

1. Awet Ayu Soap

The finest quality herbs are used to produce these finest natural herbal soaps. Awet Ayu soaps deeply cleanse and rejuvenates the skin.

LULUR HERBAL SOAP (Morning)

This soap is prepared with the highest quality ingredients, fortified with lulur (a combination of Southeast Asian herbs), which tightens and prevents the skin from wrinkling. The essence, when applied to the entire body, creates softer, luxurious skin. This soap is best used in the morning for overall protection.

MANGIR HERBAL SOAP (Evening)

This soap is prepared with the highest quality ingredients, fortified with mangir (a combination of Southeast Asian herbs) to soften and cleanse the skin. This soap contains herbal moisturizer that generates healthy skin and imparts a youthful freshness. This soap is best used in the evening.

2. Awet Ayu Shampoo

These herbal shampoos are specially formulated to care for hair, making it more manageable and silky clean. Use the appropriate Awet Ayu Shampoo according to the characteristic and condition of hair.

ALOE VERA HERBAL SHAMPOO

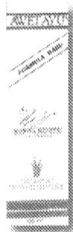

This shampoo is formulated for normal to dry hair and fortified with aloe vera. When used regularly, it restores lustre and conditions dry hair, leaving your hair more beautiful and manageable.

MERANG HERBAL SHAMPOO

This shampoo is formulated for normal to oily hair and fortified with merang, a special herb from Southeast Asia. When used regularly, it deeply cleans the scalp, ridding it of excessive oil and controlling dandruff. It leaves your hair shiny and healthy.

EGG PROTEIN HERBAL SHAMPOO

This shampoo is formulated for normal to dry and damaged hair. Fortified with egg protein and traditional herbal mixtures, it repairs and conditions brittle and heat-damaged hair, leaving it shiny, healthy and more manageable.

3. Awet Ayu Conditioner
CAMOMILE CONDITIONER

This conditioner is formulated for normal to dry hair. When used with the appropriate shampoo, the camomile within restores and revitalizes hair, leaving it healthy, lustrous, and more manageable.

4. Awet Ayu Body Lotion
ALOE VERA BODY LOTION

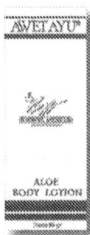

This herbal lotion is made from the finest quality aloe vera which moisturizes and keeps skin fresh and smooth. Use daily for soft and luxuriant skin.

MANGIR BODY LOTION

This herbal lotion is made from special Southeast Asian herbs to effectively moisturize the skin. Its unique composition of natural herbs deeply penetrate the skin, making it soft and silky. This special formula has a delicate fragrance. Apply daily for a fresh, smooth, and radiant look.

AWET AYU CLEANSING MILK

Awet Ayu Cleansing Milk moistens and softens while cleansing the face off dust and traces of make-up. Using your finger-tips, apply Awet Ayu Cleansing Milk to the face and neck with circular movements and remove with a cotton pad. Follow with Awet Ayu Aloe Tonic Lotion for normal to dry skin or Awet Ayu Witch Hazel Tonic Lotion for oily skin.

AWET AYU ALOE TONIC LOTION

For normal to dry skins
Awet Ayu Aloe Tonic Lotion cleanses and closes the pores whilst purifying the skin. Use especially after Awet Ayu Cleansing Milk. Apply with a cotton pad dipped in the lotion.

AWET AYU WITCH HAZEL TONIC LOTION

For oily skin
Awet Ayu Witch Hazel Tonic Lotion cleanses and closes pores while purifying the skin. Use especially after Awet Ayu Cleansing Milk. Apply with a cotton pad dipped in the lotion.

AWET AYU BUSTE CREAM

Beauty cream contains turtle oil which is useful to form lovely breasts; strengthens, and smoothens the skin while restoring sagging breasts to firm and youthful shape.

AWET AYU MANGIR SERBUK

Awet Ayu Mangir Serbuk is made from flowers and materials which are useful to keep the skin lovely and smooth.

III. HERBS FOR FAMILY CARE

A. For Mother and Baby
No. 27 JAMU NIFAS

(herbs for puerperium)
For women who have just given birth, these herbs are helpful in cleansing blood leftover in the uterus. Alleviates colic and cleanses blood. It may also be used prior to the onset of menstruation as it acts as a cycle regulator. (also available in pills)

No. 27 B JAMU NIFAS B

(herbs for regular menstrual cycle)
For women who experience late periods. Regulates menstruation and promotes proper functioning of the uterus. This herbal formula should NOT be used if pregnancy is suspected.

No. 28 JAMU SOROK I

(herbs for morning sickness and fatigue)
Special herbs for women during their first five months of pregnancy. A most effective health-aid for both mother and fetus. Alleviates fatigue, morning sickness, lack of appetite, and various pains.

No. 28 A JAMU SOROK II

(herbs for extra strength or preparation for delivery)
To be used by women from their sixth month of pregnancy
until delivery. In addition to the remedial properties of
Sorok I, this formula gives extra strength for the body to
draw upon during labor.

No. 41 JAMU GALIAN PAREM

(herbs for after childbirth)
Should be taken by women following childbirth.
Regulates blood circulation, strengthens the kidney,
cleanses the blood, and increases the production of
mother's milk. It also makes the body fit and keeps the
face radiant.

No. 47 JAMU SAWANAN

(herbs for children and nursing mothers)
For children afflicted by epilepsy, asthma, convulsions,
and other spastic disorders. For mothers still nursing, the
taking of this jamu is extremely beneficial for the health
of both mother and baby.

No. 73 PILIS SINGGUL

(herbal poultice for dizziness related to childbirth)
These herbs are to be mixed with water and applied to
the head of women after having given birth. Eliminate
dizziness, clear vision, and prevent over-production of
white blood cells.

No. 74 TAPEL RATUS

(herbal poultice for after delivery)
Herbal flakes that are made into a poultice for women.
To be taken thirty days after childbirth for the care of the
stomach, uterus, and skin.

No. 75 TAPEL SOSOK

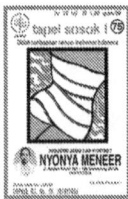

(herbal poultice for after delivery)
Apply to the mother's abdomen after giving birth for
seventeen days. Has a warming and strengthening effect
on the stomach and uterus. Helps to firm the skin and
alleviate gastric pains.

No. 76 TAPEL SIRIH

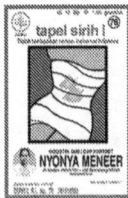

(herbal poultice for post-partum ailments)
A very effective poultice for women, to be taken seven days
after giving birth. Eases post-delivery pains and injuries
while restoring the uterus to its normal condition and
function.

No. 90 A JAMU KERING ISTIMEWA

(herbal contraceptive)
A special preparation used as a contraceptive that greatly
reduces a woman's fertility.
(also available in pills)

No. 98 JAMU SLAPAN

(herbs for after delivery)
Women should take these herbs for forty days after childbirth. Slims the stomach, strengthens the uterus, and promotes general health.

JAMU HABIS BERSALIN

(herbal set for mother and child, post-partum)
Convenient set of herbal products for women who just gave birth. There are two kinds of this jamu, which should be taken consecutively:
1. To be taken from the delivery until the 20th day after.
2. To be taken from the 20th day after up to the 40th day after.

JAMU HABIS BERSALIN ISTIMEWA

(herbal set for internal and external care)
Special set of herbs to be taken internally and others to be used externally as poultices to promote the health of mother and child following childbirth.

JAMU HABIS BERSALIN LENGKAP SUPER

(complete herbal set for internal and external care)
Contains various herbs to aid the production of mother's milk, fight debility, strengthen the stomach, abdomen, and uterus, ease muscle cramps and pains, and provide needed nutrients to both mother and baby.

No. 107 MINYAK TELON

(herbal oil for babies)
Minyak Telon is good to help eliminate puffiness and to warm babies' body. Use this oil everyday especially after a bath and during cool weather.

No. 121 MINYAK TELON SI MUNGIL

(herbal oil for toddlers)
Minyak Telon Si Mungil is good for toddlers to help eliminate puffiness and to warm their body. Use this oil everyday especially after a bath and during cool weather.

B. Herbs to Enhance Sexual Intimacy
No. 3 JAMU SEHAT PERKASA

(herbs for male virility)
Excellent for men who experience enervation, shortness of breath, and who suffer backaches from sex. Promotes general well-being and resistance to disease. Especially enhances sexual relationship by revitalizing the man's virility.
(also available in pills and capsules)

No. 3 C SEHAT PERKASA CREAM

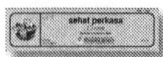

(herbal cream for male sexual potency)
Especially for men who experience difficulties in performing sexually. Contains turtle oil and is useful to increase stamina and a man's self-confidence.

No. 3 G JAMU SEHAT PERKASA + GINSENG

(herbs with ginseng for male virility)
Especially for men, one of the strongest mixtures of herbs using natural ginseng and pasak bumi that boosts testosterone levels. Excellent for men who lack energy, are short of breath, and experience backaches during sex. Especially useful to restore the strength and stamina for sexual relationship. Take regularly to increase the power of the body and to maintain youthfulness.
(also available in capsules)

No. 16 JAMU GALIAN RAPET

(herbs to enhance female sexual pleasures)
Prepared from select ingredients and made especially for
women who care for her body and appearance. Refreshes
the body, keeping it healthy, fit, and trim, and gives
the face a radiant look. Very effective in increasing the
woman's pleasures in sex as it tightens the vagina walls.
(also available in pills and capsules)

No. 52 JAMU GALIAN DELIMA PUTIH

(herbs for female youthfulness)
Herbs for older women who want retain a youthful and
attractive appearance.
(also available in pills)

No. 86 JAMU TRESNASIH

(herbs for female sex appeal)
For women who desire to maintain a passionate physical
relationship with their partner. Keeps the body youthful,
fresh, and attractive. Especially good when taken
following childbirth.
(also available in pills and capsules)

No. 103 JAMU SRIKATON

(slimming herbs)
Gives special care to the mother's body after giving
birth. Strengthens the uterus, prevents vaginal discharge,
regulates blood circulation, slims the stomach and
waistline, and keeps the face looking radiant.
(also available in pills)

IV. HERBS FOR MEN

No. 1 JAMU PRIA JANOKO

(herbs for athletes)
Specially formulated for athletes and men who work hard and enjoy an active life. Stimulates blood circulation and keeps the body strong, fit, and healthy.

No. 2 JAMU BINA TENAGA

(herbs for energy)
For men suffering from anemia and who tire easily. Treats dizziness, blackouts, clammy hands and feet, and arthritic pains. This herbal formula increases the body's energy and fights fatigue.

No. 19 JAMU PRIA SEHAT

(herbs to eliminate fatigue)
For the male body to stay strong and healthy. These herbs renew vigor and ensure a good night's sleep for those who work hard.

No. 89 JAMU LANGSING

(slimming herbs)
Slimming, health-giving herbs for overweight men.

No. 91 JAMU KLINGSIR

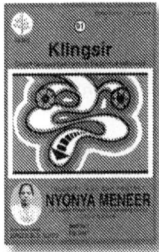

(herbs for hernias)
Herbs for the treatment of hernias.

V. HEALTH-PROMOTING HERBS

No. 14 JAMU CABE PUYANG

(herbs to renew strength)
To overcome debility and exhaustion and to help those in convalescence. Increases appetite and aids digestion.

No. 21 JAMU CARANG BURUNG

(herbs for energy)
For those suffering from impaired health, various anemic symptoms, lethargy, exhaustion, and constipation.

No. 22 JAMU SELINJONG

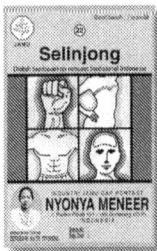

(herbs for blood circulation)
Assists in regulating blood circulation. Most effective for those who lack energy and for men and women of advanced age who constantly feel tired and have trouble sleeping.

No. 25 JAMU BERAS KENCUR

(herbs to eliminate fatigue)
To promote general health, invigorate the body, and aid blood circulation. Prepared from specially selected spices, leaves, and roots.

No. 35 SERBAT HARUM MANIS

(sweet herbal beverage)
A delicious, sweet, warm, and fragrant beverage prepared from herbs that refreshes and invigorates the body after exercise. Aids alertness and the ability to stay awake. This drink is a healthy alternative to coffee or tea.

No. 63 JAMU SEGER

(herbs to help in weight gain)
For those who need to gain weight. Makes the body strong and healthy, increases appetite and improves sleep, aids digestion, and maintains regular bowel movements.

No. 65 PARAM KOCOK

(herbal lotion for body-aches)
Selected roots and spices have been used to prepare this creamy lotion that has a soothing and curative effect when applied to swollen parts of the body, muscle strains and sprains, neuralgic and rheumatic pains, cold feet and hands. It is especially useful for women following childbirth, athletes and other active people after strenuous work, and those recovering from illness.

No. 66 PARAM MUSTIKA

(herbal compress for body-aches)
*A specially compressed ball of herbs having the same
qualities as Param Kocok. One should soften these herbs
with water before applying them to swollen and sore parts
of the body.*

No. 79 MINYAK CACAP RAMBUT

(oil for hair growth)
*Cacap Rambut Hair Oil is made of ingredients effective
for stimulating hair growth.*

No. 83 JAMU TEMULAWAK

*For the care of the stomach and kidneys. Facilitates
urination.*
(also available in bottled drink and capsules)

No. 109 JAMU SINGKIR ANGIN

(herbs for cold symptoms)
*This jamu is effective to relieve cold symptoms, such as
headaches, fevers, debility, and queasiness. It is good for
keeping the body healthy and fresh while working hard
and traveling.*
(also available in pills and capsules)

No. 109 A MINYAK SINGKIR ANGIN

(herbal oil for cold symptoms)
This oil is effective to alleviate headaches, stomachaches, and other cold symptoms.

No. 109 B BALSAM SINGKIR ANGIN

(herbal balm for cold symptoms)
This formula is effective to relieve headaches, stomachaches, and other cold symptoms.

No. 109 C PARAM KOCOK SINGKIR ANGIN EKSTRA HANGAT

(extra strength herbal balm for cold symptoms)
This formula assists in eliminating cold symptoms, stiffness, and fatigue after strenuous physical activities. Param Kocok Singkir Angin is also used to increase blood circulation, which will help people who have difficulty sleeping.

No. 109 G JAMU SINGKIR ANGIN + GINSENG

(herbs for cold symptoms)
Contains the same cold healing benefits as Jamu Singkir Angin, but with the added benefits of ginseng. Ginseng adds freshness and new vigor to this formula, which will help sustaining the body during continuous traveling and hard work.
(also available in capsules)

VI. MEDICINAL HERBS

No. 6 JAMU WASIR

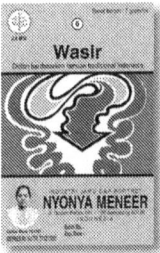

(herbs for hemorrhoids)
Relieves the pain and itching of both internal and external hemorrhoids.

No. 7 JAMU KEMANTUS

(herbs for coughs)
Herbal treatment for illnesses characterized by chronic cough, fever, chest congestion, insomnia, cold sweats, and overall debility.

No. 8 JAMU SESAK NAPAS

(herbs for asthma relief)
For the relief of asthma, chronic cough, and tuberculosis. Fights enervation and the body's susceptibility to chills.

No. 12 JAMU SARABAN

(acne prevention herbs)
Special herbs that cleanse the blood and help prevent acne and other skin problems.

No. 15 JAMU SEKALOR

(herbs for neural complaints)
Treatment for neural complaints involving headaches, dizziness, fever, exhaustion, blurred vision, watery eyes, drowsiness, and weakness.

No. 20 JAMU NGERES LINU

(herbs for body-aches)
For both men and women. A remedy for body-aches, especially lower back pains; also good for insomnia, fatigue, and restlessness.
(also available in pills and capsules)

No. 20 G JAMU NGERES LINU + GINSENG

(herbs with ginseng for body-aches)
Made from real ginseng and selected raw materials, especially formulated for muscle pains, body aches, insomnia, and painful joints. If taken regularly will increase blood circulation, refresh and revitalize the body.
(also available in capsules)

No. 23 JAMU STROONG

(herbs for flu symptoms)
Treatment for influenza symptoms, such as sore throat, earaches, headaches, watery eyes, dizziness, body aches, chills, and chapped lips.

No. 24 JAMU TUJUH ANGIN

(herbs for dizziness/nausea)
These herbs help relieve dizziness, nausea, breathing difficulties, gastric upsets, cold sweats, sore throats, fever, and suffocation.

No. 29 JAMU JAMPI USUS

(herbs for stomach ulcers)
For men and women suffering from stomach ulcers. These herbs treat diarrhea, indigestion, colic, poor appetite, and halitosis. They strengthen the stomach walls and aid digestion.

No. 31 JAMU KEMANDEN

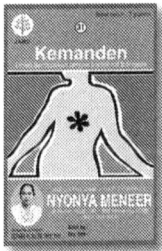

(herbs for body-aches)
For body aches that appear suddenly, accompanied by stabbing chest pains, ringing ears, and dizziness.

No. 32 JAMU BATUK

(herbal cough medicine)
For the relief of both chronic and temporary coughs.

No. 33 JAMU ENDEK-ENDEK CACING

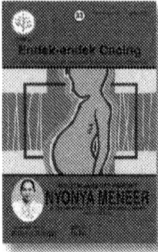

(herbal dewormer for children)
For children with worms. Signs of this condition are constant crying, facial pallor, repeated bowel movements with offensive odor, drowsiness, and halitosis.

No. 34 JAMU SARIAWAN

(herbs for various kinds of ulcers)
A herbal remedy for various kinds of ulcers. Treats ulcerated gums and mouth, throat ulcers, cold sores, stinging and watery eyes, earaches, and thrush.

No. 36 JAMU SELOKARANG

(herbs for cold symptoms)
To remedy headaches, neuralgic pains, cold, sore throat, sore muscles, and nasal complaints.

No. 37 JAMU BERSIH DARAH

(herbs to help treat venereal disease)
For the treatment of venereal and blood diseases.

No. 38 JAMU DEMAM

(herbs to help treat malaria)
To help treat the symptoms of malaria such as alternating
fever with chills, sore muscles, body aches, and cracked
lips.

No. 39 JAMU MEJEN

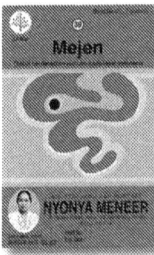

(herbs to help treat dysentery)
Combination of herbal ingredients to treat symptoms
of dysentery, such as loose bowel movements, which
sometimes contain mucous and blood, abdominal cramps,
lower back pains, colic, and gastric upset.

No. 45 JAMU SAKIT PINGGANG

(herbs for complaints related to the kidney)
Treats kidney ailments, including lower back pains,
fatigue, dizziness, insomnia, headaches, and puffy eyes;
improves kidney function.
(also available in pills)

No. 46 JAMU JAMPI SENI

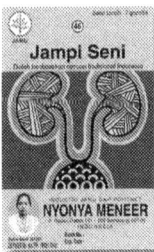

(herbs to help treat diabetes)
For the treatment of diabetes.

No. 47 JAMU SAWANAN

(herbs for children with asthma)
For children afflicted by epilepsy, asthma, convulsions and
other spastic disorders. For nursing mothers, taking of this
jamu is extremely beneficial for the health of both mother
and baby.

No. 53 JAMU SEHAT PARU

(herbs to help treat tuberculosis and debility)
This jamu helps treat tuberculosis, coughing mixed with
blood, asthma, and fatigue. It is also useful for people
who are tired and short-tempered. When taking this
jamu, it is advised to have plenty of rest.

No. 54 JAMU TUJUH LAOS

(herbs for insomnia and painful joints)
For both men and women who suffer from insomnia and
complaints of rheumatism, such as painful backs and
joints.
(also available in pills)

No. 56 JAMU GATAL-GATAL

(herbs for skin problems)
Treatment for irritating and itchy inflammations,
pimples due to rashes, chapped skin and dermatitis.
Effective in treating other diseases caused by impurities in
the blood stream.

No. 57 JAMU SAKIT KENCING

(herbs for urinary tract or bladder infection)
For bladder infection and other urinary problems, some
of which may be caused by venereal diseases.

No. 59 JAMU KENCING BATU

(herbs for kidney problems)
Effective in the treatment of kidney stones. Helps the
kidneys to function properly and cleanses the bladder and
urethra area.

No. 60 JAMU AWET ARUM

(herbal deodorant)
Acts as a natural deodorant for the body, freshens breath,
and also controls perspiration.

No. 62 JAMU PENENANG

(herbs to treat nervous disorders)
For both men and women who work hard and sometimes
have difficulty in concentrating, are quick-tempered and
have problems with heavy throbbing of the heart and
excessive perspiration. These herbs should be taken every
morning and evening to calm the nerves and stabilize the
body's system.
(also available in pills)

No. 62 A JAMU KETEGANGAN

(herbs for high blood pressure)
Herbal treatment for high blood pressure. Should be taken every morning and evening to reduce hypertension.
(also available in pills and capsules)

No. 84 JAMU BERI-BERI

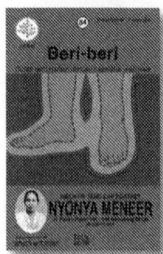

(herbs to treat beriberi)
To treat beriberi, characterized by paralysis of the extremities and emaciation.

No. 104 JAMU SAKIT MAAG

(herbs for stomach ulcers)
Herbs for the treatment of stomach ulcers.

No. 105 JAMU AKAS JANTUNG

(herbs for heart ailments)
Treats various coronary problems, such as heavy throbbing of the heart, chest pains, shortness of breath, dizziness, excessive perspiration, and insomnia.

LIST OF COURT CASES

❧

In the long history of Nyonya Meneer, there have been many internal conflicts which resulted in lawsuits such as:

1. On November 21, 1995, shareholder Tony Herlambang sued the company and the management under President Director Charles Saerang. The core of the matter: the transfer of shares by gift, done by Charles, was considered in violation of the company's articles of association. Thus, Tony demanded a change in management.

    The District Court of Semarang issued a preliminary decision, suspending the management and granting a change by placing Tony Herlambang as Director I.

    However, on June 21, 1996, as final decision, the District Court of Semarang rejected the lawsuit by Tony Herlambang in its entirety and annulled their previous preliminary decision.

Tony Herlambang appealed to the High Court of Central Java. The High Court, on December 26, 1996, upheld the District Court's decision.

Tony Herlambang appealed to the Supreme Court on February 13, 1997. However, before the cassation process began, the two parties agreed to settle.

2. On January 14, 1997, Oke Saerang, the sole distributor of Nyonya Meneer for Jakarta, Bogor, Tangerang, and Bekasi areas filed a lawsuit against the company, Agus Sulistyo, and Hadi Chandra in relation to the damages suffered due to Nyonya Meneer's appointing a new distributor. Oke Saerang sued to the company to the tune of Rp 9.5 billion (around US$3.3 million at that time) and asked for a preliminary security attachment.

    On that matter, the District Court of Central Jakarta on November 25, 1997 decided against the plaintiff and had him pay the court costs.

    On March 20, 1998, Oke Saerang appealed to the High Court of Jakarta. They decided in support of the District Court of Central Jakarta.

    On April 5, 1999, Oke Saerang appealed to the Supreme Court. Until the time of printing, the case is still in the process of examination at the Supreme Court appeal level.

3. On April 10, 1997, Nyonya Meneer represented by the owners of 1/10 of total shares, Nonie Saerang, Juliana A., and Sylviajanti S. sued Charles Saerang, Gwyneth Roberts, Oke Saerang, Vera Saerang, Fiona Oni Saerang, Alex Rumokoy, Elly M., and Amin. The core of the lawsuit is, since Nyonya Meneer's shares can only be owned by family members, the

transfer of shares by gift done by Charles, Vera, Gwyneth, and Fiona to non-family members was considered in direct violation of the company's articles of association.

The court issued a preliminary decision as follows: suspend the management with Charles Saerang as Director I, Gwyneth Roberts as Director II, and Oke Saerang, Vera Saerang, and Fiona Oni Saerang as Commissioners and appoint temporary management with Paul Saerang as Director, Peter Saerang and Lindawaty Suryadinata as Commissioners.

As final decision, however, the court decided that the preliminary decision had no legal power and rejected the plaintiff's appeal in perpetuity.

The plaintiff appealed to the High Court of Jakarta, and the court upheld the District Court's decision.

4. In 1997, Tony Herlambang as a shareholder of Nyonya Meneer filed a lawsuit against Charles Saerang as President Director of Nyonya Meneer on the suspicions of embezzlement to benefit PT Pancasan Tirta Alami.

    From 1997 to October 1998, the plaintiff repeatedly submitted case files to the High Court of Jakarta. The court studied the briefcase, determining that there wasn't enough material to proceed to trial.

5. On October 21, 1997, another internal conflict occurred. The company Nyonya Meneer filed a suit against the heirs of the late Oke Saerang as former distributor, in relation to a trade debt in the amount of Rp 1,020,732,981 (around US$350,000 at that time), which still had a balance of Rp 50,907,981 (around US$17,500). The company intended to take possession of shares in order to pay the balance. The District Court of Central

Jakarta, on October 31, 1997, decided to take over 12 shares from Nonie Saerang, 6 shares from Tony Herlambang, 6 shares from Peter Saerang, and 6 shares from Paul Saerang.

On July 28, 1998, the District Court of Central Jakarta issued further decision: granting the complaint in part and declaring the preliminary security attachment to be lawful and in effect, based on the Minutes of Preliminary Security Attachment Transcript No.08/SJ/Del.97. The court found that the defendants, the heirs of Oke Saerang, had breached their obligations.

The heirs of Oke Saerang appealed to the High Court of Jakarta on August 4, 1998. The court decided on December 13, 1999 in support of the District Court. Still unsatisfied, the heirs of Oke Saerang appealed to the Supreme Court. The case is still in the process of cassation.

6. On April 9, 1998, shareholder Paul Saerang was sued by the Public Prosecutor in relation to the slander in relation to the media announcement of a preliminary decision no.137 (see case 3 above). Paul Saerang's announcing of the illegitimate management change, which suspended Charles Saerang as President Director, yet appointed Charles' wife, Lindawaty Suryadinata, as Commissioner, made it seem that the couple had marital problems.

The court decided that Paul Saerang violated chapter 263 article 1 of the Criminal Code, but the action itself was not criminal in nature. The defendant was freed of all charges.

The Public Prosecutor appealed to the Supreme Court on November 11, 1998, but the Supreme Court denied the appeal.

7. On July 19, 1998, the company Nyonya Meneer presented its intention to dismiss Paul Saerang as the Manager of Traditional Production to the Committee for the Resolution of Labor Affairs' Disputes (*Panitia Penyelesaian Perselisihan Perburuhan* – P4P), Semarang. The reason for the dismissal was Paul Saerang's announcing of an illegitimate management change, which suspended Charles Saerang as President Director, yet appointed Charles' wife, Lindawaty Suryadinata, as Commissioner, making it seem that the couple had marital problems.

P4P Semarang refused the company's wish to dismiss Paul Saerang and instructed Paul Saerang to resume work in 14 days the latest. If fail to fulfill this condition, Paul Saerang would be considered to have resigned. The court also instructed Nyonya Meneer to pay wages to Paul Saerang from December 1997 to May 1998 in the amount of Rp 121,500,000 (around US$15,000 at that time).

Nyonya Meneer then appealed to P4P Jakarta on January 27, 1999. On May 20, 1999 P4P granted the permission for Nyonya Meneer to dismiss Paul Saerang on May 31, 1999 with a severance pay in the amount of Rp 292,950,000 (around US$33,000 at that time).

On August 2, 1999, Nyonya Meneer put forward a new demand to the State Administrative Court to be permitted to dismiss Paul Saerang without conditions.

On March 20, 2000 the court rejected Nyonya Meneer's appeal and instructed the company to pay the court costs.

The company appealed to the Supreme Court on April 7, 2000 and to the present the case remains under examination in the Supreme Court appeal level.

9. Nonie Saerang, Juliana A., Aristotle Saerang, Tony Herlambang, Paul Saerang, Sylviajanti, and Sergei O. Saerang filed a suit on December 8, 1998 against Charles Saerang, Gwyneth Roberts, Vera Saerang, Fiona Oni Saerang, Lindawaty, Henderi, Alex L., Elly Marzuki, Amin, PT Bumitra, PT Megatra, Bank Universal, Notary Juliana, the Minister of Justice, the head of office of the Department of Industry and Trade, and the State Printing Company.

   The core of the suit was the conduct in violation of the preliminary decision no.137. Charles held the general meeting of shareholders on August 29, 1997, and then on January 7 and 23, 1998, and August 31, 1998. The notarial files as well as all the entailed documents, letter of decision from the Minister of Health, Proof of Company Registration, and Addendum to the State Gazette were perceived legally defective.

   However, on February 19, 1999, the plaintiff filed an application for cancellation of the suit. The District Court of Central Jakarta decided on March 8, 1999, granting the application for cancellation.

10. The company Nyonya Meneer represented by the 1/10 of shareholders, Peter Saerang, Tony Herlambang, Aristotle Saerang, and Claus Michael Saerang filed a suit against Charles Saerang, Gwyneth Saerang, Harry Mardjono, Fiona Oni Saerang, Vera Saerang, Bank Universal, Notary Juliana Kartini Sutjendro, and the Minister of Justice, at the District Court of Central Jakarta.

    The plaintiffs questioned the legitimacy of Extraordinary General Shareholders Meeting no.9, dated January 7, 1998 (on capitalization). According to the plaintiffs, the meeting should have been cancelled because the invitation was sent only 15 days prior, instead of the customary 3 months prior. The plaintiffs also questioned the legitimacy of the Extraordinary General Shareholders Meeting no.69 dated January 23, 1998 (on the revision of the articles of association) because bribe money was involved.

On June 17, 1999 the court found that the Extraordinary General Shareholders Meeting had received the approval of the Justice Ministry and the Addendum to the State Gazette. As so, the District Court has no authority over this case, as it is more in the authority of the State Administrative Court.

The plaintiffs appealed to the High Court of Jakarta, but the court decided in support of the District Court and in favor of Charles Saerang.

NYONYA MENEER

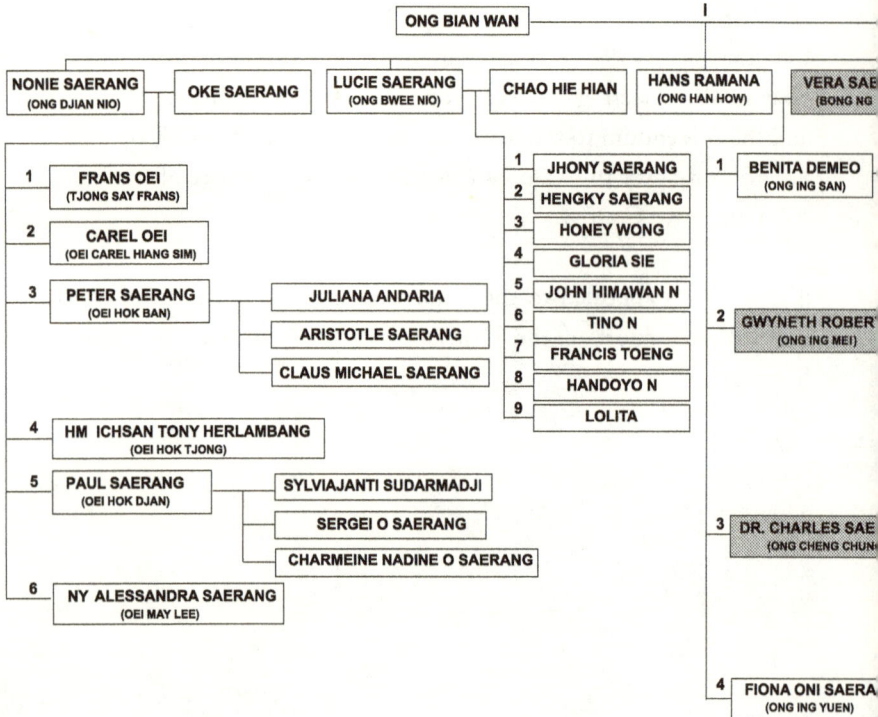

ONG BIAN WAN

NONIE SAERANG
(ONG DJIAN NIO)

OKE SAERANG

LUCIE SAERANG
(ONG BWEE NIO)

CHAO HIE HIAN

HANS RAMANA
(ONG HAN HOW)

VERA SAE
(BONG NG

1 **FRANS OEI**
(TJONG SAY FRANS)

2 **CAREL OEI**
(OEI CAREL HIANG SIM)

3 **PETER SAERANG**
(OEI HOK BAN)

- **JULIANA ANDARIA**
- **ARISTOTLE SAERANG**
- **CLAUS MICHAEL SAERANG**

4 **HM ICHSAN TONY HERLAMBANG**
(OEI HOK TJONG)

5 **PAUL SAERANG**
(OEI HOK DJAN)

- **SYLVIAJANTI SUDARMADJI**
- **SERGEI O SAERANG**
- **CHARMEINE NADINE O SAERANG**

6 **NY ALESSANDRA SAERANG**
(OEI MAY LEE)

1 **JHONY SAERANG**
2 **HENGKY SAERANG**
3 **HONEY WONG**
4 **GLORIA SIE**
5 **JOHN HIMAWAN N**
6 **TINO N**
7 **FRANCIS TOENG**
8 **HANDOYO N**
9 **LOLITA**

1 **BENITA DEMEO**
(ONG ING SAN)

2 **GWYNETH ROBER**
(ONG ING MEI)

3 **DR. CHARLES SAE**
(ONG CHENG CHUN

4 **FIONA ONI SAERA**
(ONG ING YUEN)

▨ = Current Shareholder

FAMILY TREE

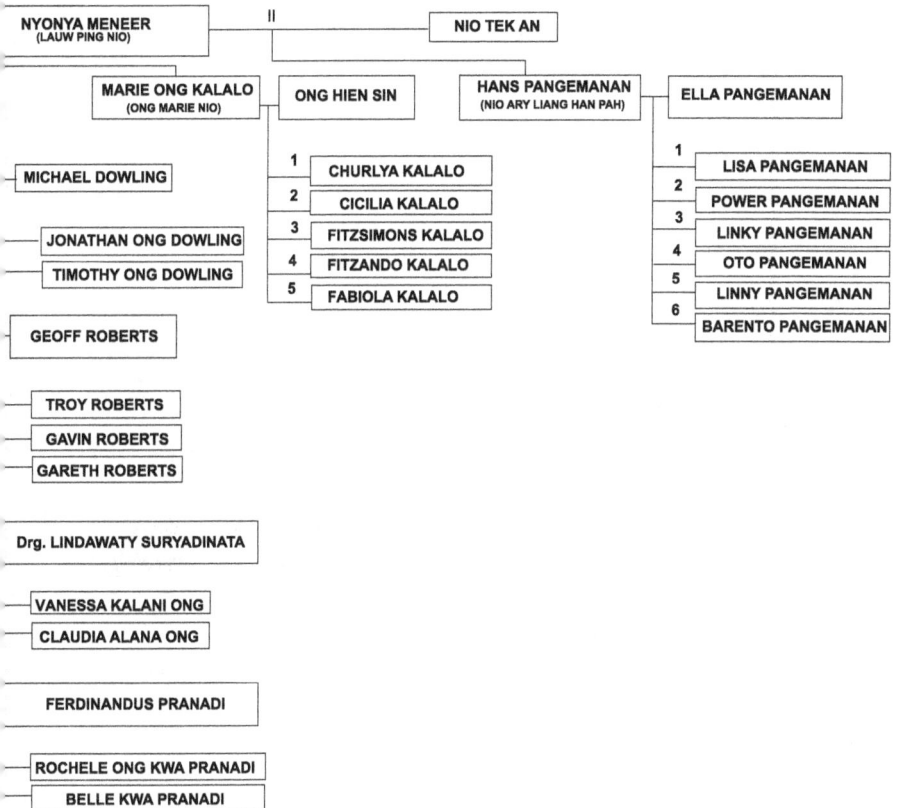

NYONYA MENEER (LAUW PING NIO) II NIO TEK AN

MARIE ONG KALALO (ONG MARIE NIO) — ONG HIEN SIN — HANS PANGEMANAN (NIO ARY LIANG HAN PAH) — ELLA PANGEMANAN

MICHAEL DOWLING

1 CHURLYA KALALO
2 CICILIA KALALO
3 FITZSIMONS KALALO
4 FITZANDO KALALO
5 FABIOLA KALALO

1 LISA PANGEMANAN
2 POWER PANGEMANAN
3 LINKY PANGEMANAN
4 OTO PANGEMANAN
5 LINNY PANGEMANAN
6 BARENTO PANGEMANAN

JONATHAN ONG DOWLING
TIMOTHY ONG DOWLING

GEOFF ROBERTS

TROY ROBERTS
GAVIN ROBERTS
GARETH ROBERTS

Drg. LINDAWATY SURYADINATA

VANESSA KALANI ONG
CLAUDIA ALANA ONG

FERDINANDUS PRANADI

ROCHELE ONG KWA PRANADI
BELLE KWA PRANADI

GLOSSARY

⁂

Ingredients commonly used in Nyonya Meneer jamu products

Adas Manis/Anise (*Pimpinella anisum*): *treats digestive problems, relieves toothache, treats influenza, lice and scabies, facilitates sleep, and freshens breath*

Adas Pedas/Fennel (*Faeniculum vulgare*): *treats chills and stomach problems, relieves croup, asthma, and bronchitis, acts as antispasmodic*

Biji Pala/Nutmeg (*Myristica fragrans*): *warms the body and facilitates sleep*

Buah Cabe Jawa/Javanese Long Pepper (*Retrofracti fructus*): *controls urine flow, regulates sweating and warms the body, functions as carminative, anti-bacterial, anti-inflammatory, anti-depressant, and stimulant, treats impotence*

Buah Kapulaga/Cardamom (*Amomi fructus*): *treats cough and prevents osteoporosis*

Buah Ketumbar/Coriander (*Coriandri fructus*): *facilitates sleep, regulates menstrual cycle, refreshes the body, acts as natural* *decongestant, calms headaches and vomiting, helps cure influenza, measles, high blood pressure, low sexual drive, and hemorrhoid, aids digestion, expels flatulence, alleviates stomachaches, increases production of mother's milk, and treats inflammation in the stomach and breasts*

Bunga Kenanga/Ylang-ylang (*Canangium flos*): *relieves high blood pressure, treats skin problems by normalizing sebum secretion, acts as natural aphrodisiac*

Bunga Sidawayah (*Woodfordiae flos*): *functions as natural astringent, helps with delivery process*

Cengkeh/Clove (*Sygyzium aromaticum*): *helps relieve digestive complaints, indigestion, flatulence, nausea, vomiting, diarrhea, functions as natural anesthetic and anti-microbial, treats cough, infertility, warts, worms, wounds, toothache, and refreshes breath*

Daun Beluntas (*Plucheae Indicae foliae*): *functions as natural anti-bacterial and anti-oxidant*

Daun Cengkeh/Clove Leaves (*Caryophylli folium*): *reduces soreness, decreases fever, stimulates sexual passion, acts as anesthetic and anti-microbial, refreshes breath, relieves toothache*

Daun Kejibeling/Red-flame (*Sericocalycis folium*): *acts as diuretic, regulates urine flow, helps digestion and defecation, helps treat hematuria (blood in urine), alleviates muscle pains, helps cure diabetes, hemorrhoid, and gallstone*

Daun Sambiloto/Green Chireta (*Andrographidis herba*): *treats diabetes, diarrhea, and hypertension, slows the spread of intestinal tumors, stimulates immune system, and acts as diuretic*

Daun Sirih/Betel Leaves (*Piperis folium*): *functions as natural antiseptic, anti-bacterial, and anti-fungal, eliminates odor and freshens the body, heals epitaxis, and helps alleviate pains from bronchitis and coughing*

Ginseng (*Panax ginseng*): *promotes energy, improves circulation, increases blood supply, revitalizes and aids recovery from weakness after illness, stimulates the body.*

Kayu Angin/Usnea or Old Man's Beard (*Usnea thallus*): *acts as antibacterial, anti-fungal, anti-tumor, antiviral, expectorant, and hemostatic*

Kayu Secang (*Sappan lignum*): *functions as anti-diarrhea, cleanses blood, rids the body of toxins, helps treat external bleeding, alleviates headaches and post-partum pains*

Kembang Sukmo (*Gunnerae flos*): *refreshes and rejuvenates the body*

Kulit Buah Pala/Nutmeg Skin (*Myristicae pericarpium*): *facilitates sleep, increases appetite, helps digestion, alleviates soreness, expels flatulence, helps with convulsions*

Kulit Kayu Rapat (*Parameriae cortex*): *decreases sweating and helps with pains after childbirth*

Kulit Pulosari (*Alyxia cortex*): *acts as carminative and antispasmodic, regulates menstrual cycle, increases appetite*

Pasak Bumi/Tongkat Ali (*Eurycoma longifolia Jack*): *boosts male libido, treats sexual dysfunctions, increases muscle strengths, helps cure hypertension, induces apoptosis in breast-cancer cells and acts as cytotoxic to lung-cancer cells, helps with post-partum injuries, functions as anti-malarial, antipyretic, anti-ulcer, and aphrodisiac*

Pegagan/Gotu Kola (*Centella herba*): *acts as anti-inflammatory, treats cough, cold, gall-ache, epistaxis, bronchitis, and dysentery, cleanses blood, facilitates urine flow, decreases fever, helps heal mouth ulcer, external wounds, keloid, and cellulitis, stimulates collagen*

Rimpang Jahe/Ginger (*Zingiberis rhizoma*): *Acts as stimulant, expectorant, and carminative, alleviates headaches and rheumatic symptoms, controls sweating, helps digestion and blood circulation*

Rimpang Kencur/Greater Galingale (*Koempferia rhizoma*): *Relieves muscle soreness, expels flatulence, acts as decongestant, rids the body of toxins, increases appetite, helps digestion, and decreases fever*

Rimpang Kunyit or Kunir/Long Turmeric Roots (*Curcumae domesticae rhizoma*): *acts as anti-inflammatory, anti-oxidant, anti-diarrhea, and pain-relieving agent, may help treat depression and some cancers; increases appetite, eases delivery process, heals colic, stops excessive bleeding, expels flatulence, imparts radiant skin, stimulates immune system*

Rimpang Laos or Rimpang Lengkuas (*Languatis rhizoma*): *neutralizes toxins, cleanses blood, helps treat convulsions and spasms, helps treat* Tinea versicolor

Rimpang Lempuyang Wangi (*Zingiberis aromaticae rhizoma*): *alleviates soreness, influenza, stomachache, anemia, malaria, and rheumatism; cleanses blood, acts as antispasmodic, increases appetite*

Rimpang Temuhitam (*Curcumae aeruginosae rhizoma*): *eases delivery process, cleanses blood, acts as carminative*

Rimpang Temukunci (*Boesenbergiae rotunda*): *helps cure diarrhea and rheumatism, acts as natural decongestant, increases appetite*

Temulawak/Round Turmeric Roots (*Curcumae rhizoma*): *treats liver problems, acts as natural anti-oxidant, anti-inflammatory, and laxative, increases appetite and stimulates the immune system, destroys kidney stone, decreases fever, helps stop external bleeding, and increases the production of mother's milk*

INDEX

OTHER TITLES BY EQUINOX PUBLISHING

NON-FICTION

SRIRO'S DESK REFERENCE OF INDONESIAN LAW 2007
Andrew I. Sriro
979-3780-48-7
2007, softcover, 672 pages

LOOSE WIRE
A Personal Guide to Making Technology Work for You
Jeremy Wagstaff
979-3780-39-8
2007, softcover, 368 pages

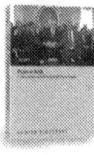

PEACE IN ACEH
A Personal Account of the Helsinki Peace Process
Damien Kingsbury
979-3780-25-8
2006, softcover, 236 pages

The Legacy of The Barang People
György Busztin
979-3780-37-1
2006, softcover, 120 pages

AT HOME ABROAD:
A Memoir of the Ford Foundation in Indonesia 1953-1973
Dewi Aggraeni
979-3780-34-7
2006, softcover, 236 pages

DREAMSEEKERS:
Indonesian Women as Domestic Workers in Asia
Dewi Aggraeni
979-3780-28-2
2006, softcover, 272 pages

THE PEPPER TRADER:
True Tales of the German East Asia Squadron and the Man who Cast them in Stone
Geoffrey Bennett
979-3780-26-6
2006, softcover, 392 pages

THE SECOND FRONT:
Inside Asia's Most Dangerous Terrorist Network
Ken Conboy
979-3780-09-6
2006, softcover, 256 pages

WARS WITHIN:
The Story of TEMPO, an Independent Magazine in Soeharto's Indonesia
Janet Steele
979-3780-08-8
2005, softcover, 368 pages

SIDELINES:
Thought Pieces from TEMPO Magazine
Goenawan Mohamad
979-3780-07-X
2005, softcover, 260 pages

AN ENDLESS JOURNEY:
Reflections of an Indonesian Journalist
Herawati Diah
979-3780-06-1
2005, softcover, 304 pages

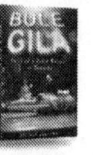

BULE GILA:
Tales of a Dutch Barman in Jakarta
Bartele Santema
979-3780-04-5
2005, softcover, 160 pages

THE INVISIBLE PALACE:
The True Story of a Journalist's Murder in Java
José Manuel Tesoro
979-97964-7-4
2004, softcover, 328 pages

INTEL: Inside Indonesia's Intelligence Service
Ken Conboy
979-97964-4-X
2004, softcover, 264 pages

KOPASSUS: Inside Indonesia's Special Forces
Ken Conboy
979-95898-8-6
2003, softcover, 352 pages

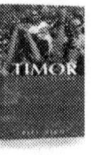

FICTION

TIMOR: A Nation Reborn
Bill Nicol
979-95898-6-X
2002, softcover, 352 pages

GUS DUR:
The Authorized Biography of Abdurrahman Wahid
Greg Barton
979-95898-5-1
2002, softcover, 436 pages

NO REGRETS: Reflections of a Presidential Spokesman
Wimar Witoelar
979-95898-4-3
2002, softcover, 200 pages

ELLIPSIS
Laksmi Pamuntjak
979-3780-30-4
2006, softcover, 98 pages

SAMAN
Ayu Utami
979-3780-11-8
2005, softcover, 184 pages

ILLUSTRATED

THE SPICE GARDEN
Michael Vatikiotis
979-97964-2-3
2004, softcover, 256 pages

THE KING, THE WITCH AND THE PRIEST
Pramoedya Ananta Toer
979-95898-3-5
2001, softcover, 128 pages

IT'S NOT AN ALL NIGHT FAIR
Pramoedya Ananta Toer
979-95898-2-7
2001, softcover, 120 pages

TALES FROM DJAKARTA
Pramoedya Ananta Toer
979-95898-1-9
2000, softcover, 286 pages

MODERN MALAYSIAN:
A Tribute to Felda's Craftspeople
Sh. Sakinah Aljunid and Warwick Purser
979-3780-32-0
2006, hardcover, 160 pages

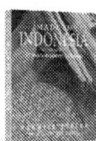

MADE IN INDONESIA:
A Tribute to the Country's
Craftspeople
Warwick Purser
979-3780-13-4
2005, hardcover, 160 pages

BANGKOK INSIDE OUT
Daniel Ziv & Guy Sharett
979-97964-6-6
2005, softcover, 176 pages

A CUP OF JAVA
Gabriella Teggia & Mark Hanusz
979-95898-9-4
2003, softcover, 144 pages

JAKARTA INSIDE OUT
Daniel Ziv
979-95898-7-8
2002, softcover, 184
pages

KRETEK:
The Culture and Heritage of
Indonesia's Clove Cigarettes
Mark Hanusz
979-95898-0-0
2006, hardcover, 224 pages

ACADEMIC

**SOCIAL SCIENCE
AND POWER IN INDONESIA**
Vedi R. Hadiz & Daniel Dhakidae
979-3780-01-0
2005, hardcover, 304 pages

**PEOPLE, POPULATION,
AND POLICY IN INDONESIA**
Terence H. Hull
979-3780-02-9
2005, hardcover, 208 pages

COMMISSIONED

**TWENTY YEARS OF
WELCOMING THE WORLD**
Melia Bali Villas
& Spa Resort
2005, hardcover, 160 pages

CELEBRATING INDONESIA:
Fifty Years with the
Ford Foundation 1953-2003
Goenawan Mohamad
979-97964-1-5
2004, hardcover, 240 pages

CLASSIC INDONESIA

**THE RISE OF INDONESIAN
COMMUNISM**
Ruth T. McVey
979-3780-36-3
2006, softcover, 510 pages

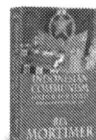

**INDONESIAN COMMUNISM
UNDER SUKARNO:**
Ideology and Politics 1959-1965
Rex Mortimer
979-3780-29-0
2006, softcover, 464 pages

**JAVA IN A TIME OF
REVOLUTION:** Occupation
and Resistance 1944-1946
Benedict R.O'G. Anderson
979-3780-14-2
2006, softcover, 516 pages

LANGUAGE AND POWER:
Exploring Political Cultures
in Indonesia
Benedict R. O'G. Anderson
979-3780-40-1
2006, softcover, 316 pages

**AN INTRODUCTION
TO INDONESIAN
HISTORIOGRAPHY**
Edited by Soedjatmoko
979-3780-44-4
2006, softcover, 468 pages

**POPULATION TRENDS
IN INDONESIA**
Widjojo Nitisastro
979-3780-43-6
2006, softcover, 292 pages

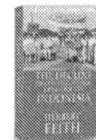

**THE DECLINE OF CONSTITUTIONAL
DEMOCRACY IN INDONESIA**
Herbert Feith
979-3780-45-2
2006, softcover, 644 pages

**MEDIA, CULTURE AND
POLITICS IN INDONESIA**
Krishna Sen and David T. Hill
979-3780-42-8
2006, softcover, 256 pages

**THE ARMY AND POLITICS
IN INDONESIA**
Harold Crouch
979-3780-50-9
2007, softcover, 592 pages

VILLAGES IN INDONESIA
Edited by Koentjaraningrat
979-3780-51-7
2007, softcover, 460 pages

**CULTURE AND POLITICS
IN INDONESIA**
Edited by Claire Holt
978-979-3780-57-3
2007, softcover, 368 pages

**INDONESIAN POLITICAL THINKING
1945-1965**
Edited by Herbert Feith
and Lance Castles
978-979-3780-52-8
2007, softcover, 524 pages

OPIUM TO JAVA:
Revenue Farming and Chinese
Enterprise in Colonial Indonesia
1860-1910
James R. Rush
979-3780-49-5
2007, softcover, 256 pages

THE ECONOMY OF INDONESIA:
Selected Readings
Edited by Bruce Glassburner
978-979-3780-55-9
2007, softcover, 460 pages

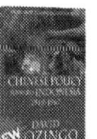

**CHINESE POLICY
TOWARD INDONESIA
1949-1967**
David Mozingo
978-979-3780-54-2
2007, softcover, 308 pages

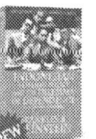

**INDONESIAN FOREIGN POLICY
AND THE DILEMMA OF
DEPENDENCE: From Sukarno
to Soeharto**
Franklin B. Weinstein
978-979-3780-56-6
2007, softcover, 388 pages